I0495722

NIST Special Publication 800-77

Guide to IPsec VPNs

Recommendations of the National Institute of Standards and Technology

Sheila Frankel
Karen Kent
Ryan Lewkowski
Angela D. Orebaugh
Ronald W. Ritchey
Steven R. Sharma

COMPUTER SECURITY

Computer Security Division
Information Technology Laboratory
National Institute of Standards and Technology
Gaithersburg, MD 20899-8930

December 2005

U.S. Department of Commerce

Carlos M. Gutierrez, Secretary

Technology Administration

Michelle O'Neill, Acting Under Secretary of Commerce for Technology

National Institute of Standards and Technology

William A. Jeffrey, Director

Acknowledgements

The authors, Sheila Frankel of the National Institute of Standards and Technology (NIST), and Karen Kent, Ryan Lewkowski, Angela D. Orebaugh, Ronald W. Ritchey, and Steven R. Sharma of Booz Allen Hamilton, wish to thank their colleagues who reviewed drafts of this document, including Bill Burr, Tim Grance, Okhee Kim, Peter Mell, and Murugiah Souppaya from NIST. The authors would also like to express their thanks to Darren Hartman and Mark Zimmerman of ICSA Labs; Paul Hoffman of the VPN Consortium; and representatives from the Department of Energy, the Department of State, the Environmental Protection Agency, and the U.S. Nuclear Regulatory Commission for their particularly valuable comments and suggestions.

Trademark Information

Table of Contents

Executive Summary ES-1

1. Introduction 1-1

1.1 Authority 1-1
1.2 Purpose and Scope 1-1
1.3 Audience 1-1
1.4 Document Structure 1-1

2. Network Layer Security 2-1

2.1 The Need for Network Layer Security 2-1
2.2 Virtual Private Networking (VPN) 2-4
2.2.1 Gateway-to-Gateway Architecture 2-5
2.2.2 Host-to-Gateway Architecture 2-6
2.2.3 Host-to-Host Architecture 2-7
2.2.4 Model Comparison 2-8
2.3 Summary 2-8

3. IPsec Fundamentals 3-1

3.1 Authentication Header (AH) 3-1
3.1.1 AH Modes 3-1
3.1.2 Integrity Protection Process 3-2
3.1.3 AH Header 3-2
3.1.4 How AH Works 3-3
3.1.5 AH Version 3 3-4
3.1.6 AH Summary 3-5
3.2 Encapsulating Security Payload (ESP) 3-5
3.2.1 ESP Modes 3-5
3.2.2 Encryption Process 3-6
3.2.3 ESP Packet Fields 3-7
3.2.4 How ESP Works 3-8
3.2.5 ESP Version 3 3-9
3.2.6 ESP Summary 3-9
3.3 Internet Key Exchange (IKE) 3-10
3.3.1 Phase One Exchange 3-10
3.3.2 Phase Two Exchange 3-15
3.3.3 Informational Exchange 3-17
3.3.4 Group Exchange 3-17
3.3.5 IKE Version 2 3-18
3.3.6 IKE Summary 3-18
3.4 IP Payload Compression Protocol (IPComp) 3-19
3.5 Putting It All Together 3-20
3.5.1 ESP in a Gateway-to-Gateway Architecture 3-20
3.5.2 ESP and IPComp in a Host-to-Gateway Architecture 3-21
3.5.3 ESP and AH in a Host-to-Host Architecture 3-22
3.6 Summary 3-23

4. IPsec Planning and Implementation 4-1

4.1 Identify Needs 4-1

4.2 Design the Solution 4-2
4.2.1 Architecture 4-3
4.2.2 Authentication 4-8
4.2.3 Cryptography 4-10
4.2.4 Packet Filter 4-10
4.2.5 Other Design Considerations 4-11
4.2.6 Summary of Design Decisions 4-13
4.3 Implement and Test Prototype 4-14
4.3.1 Component Interoperability 4-16
4.3.2 Security of the Implementation 4-18
4.4 Deploy the Solution 4-18
4.5 Manage the Solution 4-19
4.6 Summary 4-19

5. Alternatives to IPsec 5-1

5.1 Data Link Layer VPN Protocols 5-1
5.2 Transport Layer VPN Protocols 5-3
5.3 Application Layer VPN Protocols 5-5
5.4 Summary 5-6

6. Planning and Implementation Case Studies 6-1

6.1 Connecting a Remote Office to the Main Office 6-1
6.1.1 Identifying Needs and Evaluating Options 6-1
6.1.2 Designing the Solution 6-3
6.1.3 Implementing a Prototype 6-4
6.1.4 Analysis 6-6
6.2 Protecting Wireless Communications 6-7
6.2.1 Identifying Needs and Evaluating Options 6-7
6.2.2 Designing the Solution 6-8
6.2.3 Implementing a Prototype 6-10
6.2.4 Analysis 6-14
6.3 Protecting Communications for Remote Users 6-14
6.3.1 Identifying Needs and Evaluating Options 6-15
6.3.2 Designing the Solution 6-16
6.3.3 Implementing a Prototype 6-18
6.3.4 Analysis 6-21

7. Future Directions 7-1

7.1 Revised IPsec Standards 7-1
7.2 Support for Multicast Traffic 7-1
7.3 Interoperability with PKI 7-2
7.4 IKE Mobility and Multihoming 7-2
7.5 IPv6 7-2

List of Appendices

Appendix A— Policy Considerations A-1
A.1 Communications with a Remote Office Network A-1
A.1.1 IPsec Gateway Devices and Management Servers A-1
A.1.2 Hosts and People Using the IPsec Tunnel A-2
A.2 Communications with a Business Partner Network A-2
A.2.1 Interconnection Agreement A-2
A.2.2 IPsec Gateway Devices and Management Servers A-4
A.2.3 Hosts and People Using the IPsec Tunnel A-4
A.3 Communications for Individual Remote Hosts A-4
A.3.1 Remote Access Policy A-4
A.3.2 IPsec Gateway Devices and Management Servers A-5
Appendix B— Case Study Configuration Files B-1
B.1 Section 6.1 Case Study B-1
B.2 Section 6.2 Case Study B-2
B.2.1 isakmpd.conf B-2
B.2.2 isakmpd.policy B-3
Appendix C— Glossary C-1
Appendix D— Acronyms D-1
Appendix E— Resources E-1
Appendix F— Index F-1

List of Figures

Figure 2-1. TCP/IP Layers 2-1
Figure 2-2. Gateway-to-Gateway Architecture Example 2-5
Figure 2-3. Host-to-Gateway Architecture Example 2-6
Figure 2-4. Host-to-Host Architecture Example 2-7
Figure 3-1. AH Tunnel Mode Packet 3-1
Figure 3-2. AH Transport Mode Packet 3-1
Figure 3-3. AH Header 3-3
Figure 3-4. Sample AH Transport Mode Packet 3-3
Figure 3-5. AH Header Fields from Sample Packet 3-4
Figure 3-6. ESP Tunnel Mode Packet 3-6
Figure 3-7. ESP Transport Mode Packet 3-6
Figure 3-8. ESP Packet Fields 3-8
Figure 3-9. ESP Packet Capture 3-8

Figure 3-10. ESP Header Fields from Sample Packets 3-9
Figure 3-11. Ethereal Interpretation of a First Pair Main Mode Message 3-13
Figure 3-12. Ethereal Interpretation of a Second Pair Main Mode Message 3-14
Figure 3-13. Ethereal Interpretation of a Third Pair Main Mode Message 3-14
Figure 3-14. Ethereal Interpretation of a Quick Mode Message 3-16
Figure 5-1. TCP/IP Layers 5-1
Figure 6-1. Gateway-to-Gateway VPN for Remote Office Connectivity 6-4
Figure 6-2. Host-to-Gateway VPN for Protecting Wireless Communications 6-9
Figure 6-3. Host-to-Gateway VPN for Protecting Communications 6-17

List of Tables

Table 2-1. Comparison of VPN Architecture Models 2-8
Table 3-1. Diffie-Hellman Group Definitions 3-12
Table 4-1. Design Decisions Checklist 4-14
Table 5-1. Comparison of IPsec and IPsec Alternatives 5-7
Table 5-2. IP Protocols and TCP/UDP Port Numbers for VPN Protocols 5-8

Executive Summary

IPsec is a framework of open standards for ensuring private communications over public networks. It has become the most common network layer security control, typically used to create a virtual private network (VPN). A VPN is a virtual network built on top of existing physical networks that can provide a secure communications mechanism for data and control information transmitted between networks. VPNs are used most often to protect communications carried over public networks such as the Internet. A VPN can provide several types of data protection, including confidentiality, integrity, data origin authentication, replay protection and access control. Although VPNs can reduce the risks of networking, they cannot totally eliminate them. For example, a VPN implementation may have flaws in algorithms or software, or a VPN may be set up with insecure configuration settings and values. Both of these flaws can be exploited by attackers. There are three primary models for VPN architectures, as follows:

- **Gateway-to-gateway.** This model protects communications between two specific networks, such as an organization's main office network and a branch office network, or two business partners' networks.
- **Host-to-gateway.** This model protects communications between one or more individual hosts and a specific network belonging to an organization. The host-to-gateway model is most often used to allow hosts on unsecured networks, such as traveling employees and telecommuters, to gain access to internal organizational services, such as the organization's e-mail and Web servers.
- **Host-to-host.** A host-to-host architecture protects communication between two specific computers. It is most often used when a small number of users need to use or administer a remote system that requires the use of inherently insecure protocols.

The guide provides an overview of the types of security controls that can provide protection for Transmission Control Protocol/Internet Protocol (TCP/IP) network communications, which are widely used throughout the world. TCP/IP communications are composed of four layers that work together: application, transport, network, and data link. Security controls exist for network communications at each of the four layers. As data is prepared for transport, it is passed from the highest to the lowest layer, with each layer adding more information. Because of this, a security control at a higher layer cannot provide full protection for lower layers, because the lower layers add information to the communications after the higher layer security controls have been applied. The primary disadvantage of lower layer security controls is that they are less flexible and granular than higher layer controls. Accordingly, network layer controls have become widely used for securing communications because they provide a more balanced solution than the highest layer and lowest layer security controls.

IPsec is a network layer security protocol with the following components:

- **Two security protocols, Authentication Header (AH) and Encapsulating Security Payload (ESP).** AH can provide integrity protection for packet headers and data, but it cannot encrypt them. ESP can provide encryption and integrity protection for packets, but it cannot protect the outermost IP header, as AH can. However, this protection is not needed in most cases. Accordingly, ESP is used much more frequently than AH because of its encryption capabilities, as well as other operational advantages which will be described in this document. For a VPN, which requires confidential communications, ESP is the natural choice.
- **Internet Key Exchange (IKE) protocol.** IPsec uses IKE to negotiate IPsec connection settings; authenticate endpoints to each other; define the security parameters of IPsec-protected connections; negotiate secret keys; and manage, update, and delete IPsec-protected communication channels.

- **IP Payload Compression Protocol (IPComp).** Optionally, IPsec can use IPComp to compress packet payloads before encrypting them.

IKE negotiates the cryptographic algorithms and related settings to be used for AH and ESP. Federal agencies are required to use Federal Information Processing Standards (FIPS) approved cryptographic algorithms specified in FIPS or in NIST Recommendations and contained in validated cryptographic modules. The Cryptographic Module Validation Program (CMVP) is a joint effort between NIST and the Communications Security Establishment (CSE) of the Government of Canada for the validation of cryptographic modules against FIPS 140-2: *Security Requirements for Cryptographic Modules*. The Advanced Encryption Standard (AES) algorithm is the strongest approved algorithm, and is the preferred algorithm for Federal agency use. The Triple Data Encryption Algorithm (TDEA), also known as Triple DES (3DES), is also an approved algorithm and is also acceptable for Federal agency use.

In addition to providing specific recommendations related to configuring cryptography for IPsec, this guide presents a phased approach to IPsec planning and implementation that can help in achieving successful IPsec deployments. The five phases of the approach are as follows:

1. **Identify Needs**—Identify the need to protect network communications and determine how that need can best be met.

2. **Design the Solution**—Make design decisions in four areas: architectural considerations, authentication methods, cryptography policy, and packet filters. The placement of an IPsec gateway has potential security, functionality, and performance implications. An authentication solution should be selected based primarily on maintenance, scalability, and security. Packet filters should apply appropriate protections to traffic and not protect other types of traffic for performance or functionality reasons.

3. **Implement and Test a Prototype**—Test a prototype of the designed solution in a lab or test environment to identify any potential issues. Testing should evaluate several factors, including connectivity, protection, authentication, application compatibility, management, logging, performance, the security of the implementation, and component interoperability.

4. **Deploy the Solution**—Gradually deploy IPsec throughout the enterprise. Existing network infrastructure, applications, and users should be moved incrementally over time to the new IPsec solution. This provides administrators an opportunity to evaluate the impact of the IPsec solution and resolve issues prior to enterprise-wide deployment.

5. **Manage the Solution**—Maintain the IPsec components and resolve operational issues; repeat the planning and implementation process when significant changes need to be incorporated into the solution.

As part of implementing IPsec, organizations should also implement additional technical, operational, and management controls that support and complement IPsec implementations. Examples include establishing control over all entry and exit points for the protected networks, ensuring the security of all IPsec endpoints, and incorporating IPsec considerations into organizational policies.

NIST's requirements and recommendations for the configuration of IPsec VPNs are:

- If any of the information that will traverse a VPN should not be seen by non-VPN users, then the VPN must provide confidentiality protection (encryption) for that information.

- A VPN must use a FIPS-approved encryption algorithm. AES-CBC (AES in Cipher Block Chaining mode) with a 128-bit key is highly recommended; Triple DES (3DES-CBC)[1] is also acceptable. The Data Encryption Standard (DES) is also an encryption algorithm; since it has been successfully attacked, it should not be used.[2]
- A VPN must always provide integrity protection.
- A VPN must use a FIPS-approved integrity protection algorithm. HMAC-SHA-1 is highly recommended. HMAC-MD5 also provides integrity protection, but it is not a FIPS-approved algorithm.
- A VPN should provide replay protection.
- For IKEv1, IKE Security Associations (SAs) should have a lifetime no greater than 24 hours (86400 seconds) and IPsec SAs should have a lifetime no greater than 8 hours (28800 seconds). For IKEv2, IKE SAs should be re-keyed after at most 24 hours and child SAs should be re-keyed after at most 8 hours.
- The Diffie-Hellman (DH) group used to establish the secret keying material for IKE and IPsec should be consistent with current security requirements. DH group 2 (1024-bit MODP) should be used for Triple DES and for AES with a 128-bit key. For greater security, DH group 5 (1536-bit MODP) or DH group 14 (2048-bit MODP) may be used for AES.[3] The larger DH groups will result in increased processing time.

---

1 Many encryption algorithms can be applied with multiple modes of operation. Within IPsec, the Cipher Block Chaining (CBC) mode is the standard mode for Triple DES; it is also commonly used with AES. In this document, the term Triple DES or 3DES will always refer to Triple DES-CBC. The term AES will refer to AES-CBC. For other AES modes (e.g. counter mode), the mode will always be explicity specified (e.g. AES-CTR).

2 NIST has withdrawn FIPS 46-3, DES, and recommends a transition to other FIPS-approved encryption algorithms.

3 As of mid-2005, all IPsec implementations include DH group 2, most include DH group 5, and very few include DH group 14.

1. Introduction

1.1 Authority

The National Institute of Standards and Technology (NIST) developed this document in furtherance of its statutory responsibilities under the Federal Information Security Management Act (FISMA) of 2002, Public Law 107-347.

NIST is responsible for developing standards and guidelines, including minimum requirements, for providing adequate information security for all agency operations and assets, but such standards and guidelines shall not apply to national security systems. This guideline is consistent with the requirements of the Office of Management and Budget (OMB) Circular A-130, Section 8b(3), "Securing Agency Information Systems," as analyzed in A-130, Appendix IV: Analysis of Key Sections. Supplemental information is provided in A-130, Appendix III.

This guideline has been prepared for use by Federal agencies. It may be used by nongovernmental organizations on a voluntary basis and is not subject to copyright, though attribution is desired.

Nothing in this document should be taken to contradict standards and guidelines made mandatory and binding on Federal agencies by the Secretary of Commerce under statutory authority, nor should these guidelines be interpreted as altering or superseding the existing authorities of the Secretary of Commerce, Director of the OMB, or any other Federal official.

1.2 Purpose and Scope

This publication seeks to assist organizations in mitigating the risks associated with the transmission of sensitive information across networks by providing practical guidance on implementing security services based on Internet Protocol Security (IPsec). This document presents information that is independent of particular hardware platforms, operating systems, and applications, other than providing real-world examples to illustrate particular concepts. Specifically, the document includes a discussion of the need for network layer security services, a description of the types of services that are offered at the network layer, and how IPsec addresses these services. It uses a case-based approach to show how IPsec can be used to solve common network security issues. It also describes alternatives to IPsec and discusses under what circumstances each alternative may be appropriate.

1.3 Audience

This document has been created for network architects, network administrators, security staff, technical support staff, and computer security program managers who are responsible for the technical aspects of preparing, operating, and securing networked infrastructures. The material in this document is technically oriented, and it is assumed that readers have at least a basic understanding of networking and network security.

1.4 Document Structure

The remainder of this document is organized into six major sections. Section 2 discusses the need for network layer security and introduces the concept of virtual private networking (VPN). Section 3 covers the fundamentals of IPsec, focusing on the protocols Encapsulating Security Payload (ESP), Authentication Header (AH), Internet Key Exchange (IKE), and IP Payload Compression Protocol (IPComp). Section 4 points out issues to be considered during IPsec planning and implementation. Section 5 discusses several alternatives to IPsec and describes when each method may be appropriate.

Section 6 presents several case studies that show how IPsec could be used in various scenarios. Section 7 briefly discusses future directions for IPsec.

The document also contains several appendices with supporting material. Appendix A discusses the needs for IPsec-related policy and provides examples of common IPsec policy considerations. Appendix B contains configuration files referenced by the case studies in Section 6. Appendices C and D contain a glossary and acronym list, respectively. Appendix E lists print and online resources that may be useful for IPsec planning and implementation. Appendix F contains an index for the guide.

2. Network Layer Security

This section provides a general introduction to *network layer security*—protecting network communications at the layer that is responsible for routing packets across networks. It first introduces the Transmission Control Protocol/Internet Protocol (TCP/IP) model and its layers, and then discusses the need to use security controls at each layer to protect communications. It provides a brief introduction to IPsec, primarily focused on the types of protection that IPsec can provide for communications. This section also provides a brief introduction to Virtual Private Networking (VPN) services and explains what types of protection a VPN can provide. It introduces three VPN architecture models and discusses the features and common uses of each model.[4]

2.1 The Need for Network Layer Security

TCP/IP is widely used throughout the world to provide network communications. TCP/IP communications are composed of four layers that work together. When a user wants to transfer data across networks, the data is passed from the highest layer through intermediate layers to the lowest layer, with each layer adding additional information.[5] The lowest layer sends the accumulated data through the physical network; the data is then passed up through the layers to its destination. Essentially, the data produced by a layer is encapsulated in a larger container by the layer below it. The four TCP/IP layers, from highest to lowest, are shown in Figure 2-1.

Application Layer. This layer sends and receives data for particular applications, such as Domain Name System (DNS), HyperText Transfer Protocol (HTTP), and Simple Mail Transfer Protocol (SMTP).
Transport Layer. This layer provides connection-oriented or connectionless services for transporting application layer services between networks. The transport layer can optionally assure the reliability of communications. Transmission Control Protocol (TCP) and User Datagram Protocol (UDP) are commonly used transport layer protocols.
Network Layer. This layer routes packets across networks. Internet Protocol (IP) is the fundamental network layer protocol for TCP/IP. Other commonly used protocols at the network layer are Internet Control Message Protocol (ICMP) and Internet Group Management Protocol (IGMP).
Data Link Layer. This layer handles communications on the physical network components. The best-known data link layer protocol is Ethernet.

Figure 2-1. TCP/IP Layers

Security controls exist for network communications at each layer of the TCP/IP model. As previously explained, data is passed from the highest to the lowest layer, with each layer adding more information. Because of this, a security control at a higher layer cannot provide full protection for lower layers, because the lower layers perform functions of which the higher layers are not aware. The following items discuss the security controls that are available at each layer:

- **Application Layer.** Separate controls must be established for each application. For example, if an application needs to protect sensitive data sent across networks, the application may need to be

4 This document discusses only the most common VPN scenarios and uses of IPsec.

5 At each layer, the logical units are typically composed of a header and a payload. The *payload* consists of the information passed down from the previous layer, while the *header* contains layer-specific information such as addresses. At the application layer, the payload is the actual application data.

modified to provide this protection. While this provides a very high degree of control and flexibility over the application's security, it may require a large resource investment to add and configure controls properly for each application. Designing a cryptographically sound application protocol is very difficult, and implementing it properly is even more challenging, so creating new application layer security controls is likely to create vulnerabilities. Also, some applications, particularly off-the-shelf software, may not be capable of providing such protection. While application layer controls can protect application data, they cannot protect TCP/IP information such as IP addresses because this information exists at a lower layer. Whenever possible, application layer controls for protecting network communications should be standards-based solutions that have been in use for some time. One example is Pretty Good Privacy (PGP), which is commonly used to encrypt e-mail messages.[6]

- **Transport Layer.** Controls at this layer can be used to protect the data in a single communication session between two hosts. Because IP information is added at the network layer, transport layer controls cannot protect it. The most common use for transport layer protocols is securing HTTP traffic; the Transport Layer Security (TLS)[7] protocol is usually used for this. The use of TLS typically requires each application to support TLS; however, unlike application layer controls, which typically involve extensive customization of the application, transport layer controls such as TLS are much less intrusive because they simply protect network communications and do not need to understand the application's functions or characteristics. Although using TLS may require modifying some applications, TLS is a well-tested protocol that has several implementations that have been added to many applications, so it is a relatively low-risk option compared to adding protection at the application layer instead. One drawback of TLS is that it is only capable of protecting TCP-based communications, as opposed to UDP, because it assumes the network layer protocol is ensuring reliability. (An alternative approach is the use of a TLS proxy server. See Section 5.2 for a discussion of this topic.)

- **Network Layer.** Controls at this layer apply to all applications and are not application-specific. For example, all network communications between two hosts or networks can be protected at this layer without modifying any applications on the clients or the servers. In many environments, network layer controls such as IPsec provide a much better solution than transport or application layer controls because of the difficulties in adding controls to individual applications. Network layer controls also provide a way for network administrators to enforce certain security policies. Another advantage of network layer controls is that since IP information (e.g., IP addresses) is added at this layer, the controls can protect both the data within the packets and the IP information for each packet. However, network layer controls provide less control and flexibility for protecting specific applications than transport and application layer controls.

- **Data Link Layer.** Data link layer controls are applied to all communications on a specific physical link, such as a dedicated circuit between two buildings or a dial-up modem connection to an Internet Service Provider (ISP). Data link layer controls for dedicated circuits are most often provided by specialized hardware devices known as data link encryptors; data link layer controls for other types of connections, such as dial-up modem communications, are usually provided through software. Because the data link layer is below the network layer, controls at this layer

---

6 Several Request for Comment (RFC) documents from the Internet Engineering Task Force (IETF) define PGP, as well as standards for using it to protect e-mail messages. One example is RFC 3156, *MIME Security with OpenPGP*, available at http://www.ietf.org/rfc/rfc3156.txt.

7 TLS is the standards-based version of Secure Sockets Layer (SSL) version 3. More information on TLS is available from the IETF Transport Layer Security working group home page at http://www.ietf.org/html.charters/tls-charter.html, and in RFC 2246, *The TLS Protocol Version 1.0*, available at http://www.ietf.org/rfc/rfc2246.txt. Another good source of information is NIST SP 800-52, *Guidelines on the Selection and Use of Transport Layer Security*, available from http://csrc.nist.gov/publications/nistpubs/.

can protect both data and IP information. Compared to controls at the other layers, data link layer controls are relatively simple, which makes them easier to implement; also, they support other network layer protocols besides IP. Because data link layer controls are specific to a particular physical link, they are poorly suited to protecting connections with multiple links, such as establishing a VPN over the Internet. An Internet-based connection is typically composed of several physical links chained together; protecting such a connection with data link layer controls would require deploying a separate control to each link, which is not feasible. Data link layer protocols have been used for many years primarily to provide additional protection for specific physical links that should not be trusted.

Because they can provide protection for many applications at once without modifying them, network layer security controls have been used frequently for securing communications, particularly over shared networks such as the Internet. Network layer security controls provide a single solution for protecting data from all applications, as well as protecting IP information. However, in many cases, controls at another layer are better suited to providing protection than network layer controls. For example, if only one or two applications need protection, a network layer control may be overkill. Controls at each layer offer advantages and features that controls at other layers do not. Information on data link, transport, and application layer alternatives to network layer controls is provided in Section 5.

Internet Protocol Security (IPsec)[8] has emerged as the most commonly used network layer security control for protecting communications. IPsec is a framework of open standards for ensuring private communications over IP networks. Depending on how IPsec is implemented and configured, it can provide any combination of the following types of protection:

- **Confidentiality.** IPsec can ensure that data cannot be read by unauthorized parties. This is accomplished by encrypting data using a cryptographic algorithm and a secret key—a value known only to the two parties exchanging data. The data can only be decrypted by someone who has the secret key.

- **Integrity.** IPsec can determine if data has been changed (intentionally or unintentionally) during transit. The integrity of data can be assured by generating a message authentication code (MAC) value, which is a cryptographic checksum of the data. If the data is altered and the MAC is recalculated, the old and new MACs will differ.

- **Peer Authentication.** Each IPsec endpoint confirms the identity of the other IPsec endpoint with which it wishes to communicate, ensuring that the network traffic and data is being sent from the expected host.

- **Replay Protection.** The same data is not delivered multiple times, and data is not delivered grossly out of order. However, IPsec does not ensure that data is delivered in the exact order in which it is sent.

- **Traffic Analysis Protection.** A person monitoring network traffic does not know which parties are communicating, how often communications are occurring, or how much data is being exchanged. However, the number of packets being exchanged can be counted.

---

8 The IPsec protocols were developed within the IPsec Working Group of the Internet Engineering Task Force (IETF). They are defined in 2 types of documents: Request for Comment (RFC), which are accepted standards; and Internet-Drafts, which are working documents that may become RFCs. The last 2 digits of the name of an Internet-Draft represent its version number (e.g., 00 or 05). Since this is subject to change, this document will substitute "xx" for the version number of referenced Internet-Drafts. A list of IPsec documents can be found at http://www.ietf.org/html.charters/OLD/ipsec-charter.html.

- **Access Control.** IPsec endpoints can perform filtering to ensure that only authorized IPsec users can access particular network resources. IPsec endpoints can also allow or block certain types of network traffic, such as allowing Web server access but denying file sharing.

2.2 Virtual Private Networking (VPN)

The most common use of IPsec implementations is providing Virtual Private Networking (VPN) services. A *VPN* is a virtual network, built on top of existing physical networks, that can provide a secure communications mechanism for data and IP information transmitted between networks. Because a VPN can be used over existing networks, such as the Internet, it can facilitate the secure transfer of sensitive data across public networks. This is often less expensive than alternatives such as dedicated private telecommunications lines between organizations or branch offices. VPNs can also provide flexible solutions, such as securing communications between remote telecommuters and the organization's servers, regardless of where the telecommuters are located. A VPN can even be established within a single network to protect particularly sensitive communications from other parties on the same network. Sections 2.2.1 through 2.2.3 discuss these three models: gateway-to-gateway, host-to-gateway, and host-to-host.

VPNs can use both symmetric and asymmetric forms of cryptography. *Symmetric cryptography* uses the same key for both encryption and decryption, while *asymmetric cryptography* uses separate keys for encryption and decryption, or to digitally sign and verify a signature. Symmetric cryptography is generally more efficient and requires less processing power than asymmetric cryptography, which is why it is typically used to encrypt the bulk of the data being sent over a VPN. One problem with symmetric cryptography is with the key exchange process; keys must be exchanged out-of-band to ensure confidentiality.[9] Common algorithms that implement symmetric cryptography include Digital Encryption Standard (DES), Triple DES (3DES), Advanced Encryption Standard (AES), Blowfish, RC4, International Data Encryption Algorithm (IDEA), and the hash message authentication code (HMAC) versions of Message Digest 5 (MD5) and Secure Hash Algorithm (SHA-1).[10]

Asymmetric cryptography (also known as *public key cryptography*) uses two separate keys to exchange data. One key is used to encrypt or digitally sign the data, and the other key is used to decrypt the data or verify the digital signature. These keys are often referred to as public/private key combinations. If an individual's public key (which can be shared with others) is used to encrypt data, then only that same individual's private key (which is known only to the individual) can be used to decrypt the data. If an individual's private key is used to digitally sign data, then only that same individual's public key can be used to verify the digital signature. Common algorithms that implement asymmetric cryptography include RSA, Digital Signature Algorithm (DSA), and Elliptic Curve DSA (ECDSA).[11]

Although there are numerous ways in which IPsec can be implemented, most implementations use both symmetric and asymmetric cryptography. Asymmetric cryptography is used to authenticate the identities of both parties, while symmetric encryption is used for protecting the actual data because of its relative efficiency.

---

9 *Out-of-band* refers to using a separate communications mechanism to transfer information. For example, the VPN cannot be used to exchange the keys securely because the keys are required to provide the necessary protection.

10 Federal agencies must use FIPS-approved encryption algorithms contained in validated cryptographic modules. The list of algorithms in this section includes algorithms such as DES and MD5 that are either no longer approved or were never approved. The Cryptographic Module Validation Program (CMVP) at NIST coordinates FIPS 140-2 testing; the CMVP Web site is located at http://csrc.nist.gov/cryptval/. See http://csrc nist.gov/cryptval/des.htm for information on FIPS-approved symmetric key algorithms. FIPS 140-2, *Security Requirements for Cryptographic Modules*, is available at http://csrc.nist.gov/publications/fips/fips140-2/fips1402.pdf.

11 FIPS-approved algorithms must also be used for digital signatures. See http://csrc nist.gov/cryptval/dss.htm for information on such algorithms.

It is important to understand that VPNs do not remove all risk from networking. While VPNs can greatly reduce risk, particularly for communications that occur over public networks, they cannot eliminate all risk for such communications. One potential problem is the strength of the implementation. For example, flaws in an encryption algorithm or the software implementing the algorithm could allow attackers to decrypt intercepted traffic; random number generators that do not produce sufficiently random values could provide additional attack possibilities. Another issue is encryption key disclosure; an attacker who discovers a key could not only decrypt traffic, but potentially also pose as a legitimate user. Another area of risk involves availability. A common model for information assurance is based on the concepts of confidentiality, integrity, and availability. Although VPNs are designed to support confidentiality and integrity, they generally do not improve *availability*, the ability for authorized users to access systems as needed. In fact, many VPN implementations actually tend to decrease availability somewhat because they add more components and services to the existing network infrastructure. This is highly dependent upon the chosen VPN architecture model and the details of the implementation. The following sections describe each of the three primary VPN architectures: host-to-host, host-to-gateway, and gateway-to-gateway.

2.2.1 Gateway-to-Gateway Architecture

IPsec-based VPNs are often used to provide secure network communications between two networks. This is typically done by deploying a VPN gateway onto each network and establishing a VPN connection between the two gateways. Traffic between the two networks that needs to be secured passes within the established VPN connection between the two VPN gateways. The VPN gateway may be a dedicated device that only performs VPN functions, or it may be part of another network device, such as a firewall or router. Figure 2-2 shows an example of an IPsec network architecture that uses the gateway-to-gateway model to provide a protected connection between the two networks.

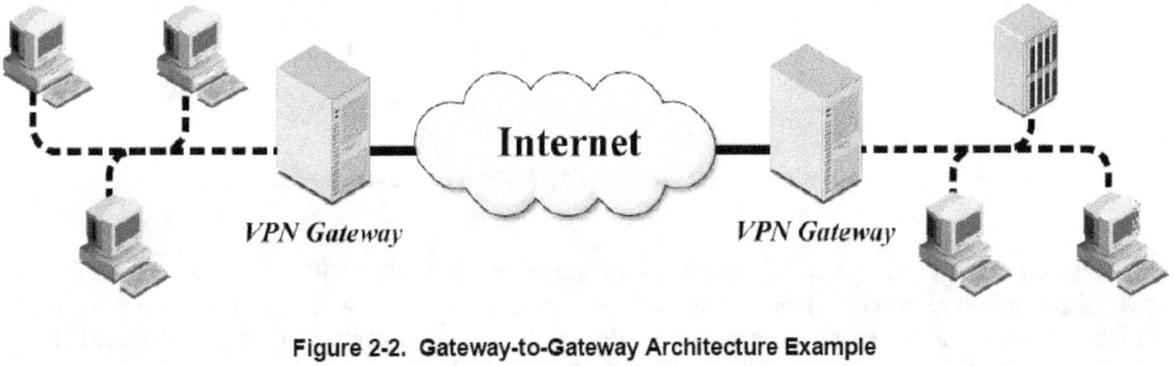

Figure 2-2. Gateway-to-Gateway Architecture Example

This model is relatively simple to understand. To facilitate VPN connections, one of the VPN gateways issues a request to the other to establish an IPsec connection. The two VPN gateways exchange information with each other and create an IPsec connection. Routing on each network is configured so that as hosts on one network need to communicate with hosts on the other network, their network traffic is automatically routed through the IPsec connection, protecting it appropriately. A single IPsec connection establishing a tunnel between the gateways can support all communications between the two networks, or multiple IPsec connections can each protect different types or classes of traffic.

Figure 2-2 illustrates that a gateway-to-gateway VPN does not provide full protection for data throughout its transit. In fact, the gateway-to-gateway model only protects data between the two gateways, as denoted by the solid line. The dashed lines indicate that communications between VPN clients and their local gateway, and between the remote gateway and destination hosts (e.g., servers) are not protected.

The other VPN models provide protection for more of the transit path. The gateway-to-gateway model is most often used when connecting two secured networks, such as linking a branch office to headquarters over the Internet. Gateway-to-gateway VPNs often replace more costly private wide area network (WAN) circuits.

The gateway-to-gateway model is the easiest to implement, in terms of user and host management. Gateway-to-gateway VPNs are typically transparent to users, who do not need to perform separate authentication just to use the VPN. Also, the users' systems and the target hosts (e.g., servers) should not need to have any VPN client software installed, nor should they require any reconfiguration, to be able to use the VPN.

2.2.2 Host-to-Gateway Architecture

An increasingly common VPN model is the host-to-gateway model, which is most often used to provide secure remote access. The organization deploys a VPN gateway onto their network; each remote access user then establishes a VPN connection between the local computer (host) and the VPN gateway. As with the gateway-to-gateway model, the VPN gateway may be a dedicated device or part of another network device. Figure 2-3 shows an example of an IPsec host-to-gateway architecture that provides a protected connection for the remote user.

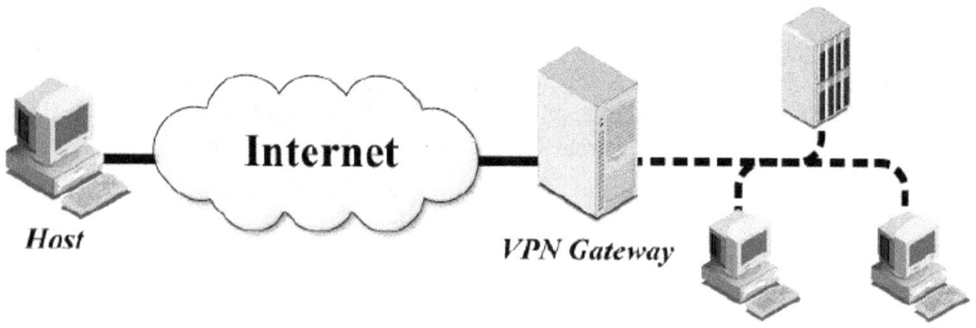

Figure 2-3. Host-to-Gateway Architecture Example

In this model, IPsec connections are created as needed for each individual VPN user. Remote users' hosts have been configured to act as IPsec clients with the organization's IPsec gateway. When a remote user wishes to use computing resources through the VPN, the host initiates communications with the VPN gateway. The user is typically asked by the VPN gateway to authenticate before the connection can be established. The VPN gateway can perform the authentication itself or consult a dedicated authentication server. The client and gateway exchange information, and the IPsec connection is established. The user can now use the organization's computing resources, and the network traffic between the user's host and the VPN gateway will be protected by the IPsec connection. Traffic between the user and systems not controlled by the organization can also be routed through the VPN gateway; this allows IPsec protection to be applied to this traffic as well if desired.

As shown in Figure 2-3, the host-to-gateway VPN does not provide full protection for data throughout its transit. The dashed lines indicate that communications between the gateway and the destination hosts (e.g., servers) are not protected. The host-to-gateway model is most often used when connecting hosts on unsecured networks to resources on secured networks, such as linking traveling employees around the world to headquarters over the Internet. Host-to-gateway VPNs often replace dial-up modem pools. The host-to-gateway model is somewhat complex to implement and maintain in terms of user and host management. Host-to-gateway VPNs are typically not transparent to users because they must authenticate before using the VPN. Also, the users' hosts need to have VPN client software configured.[12]

2.2.3 Host-to-Host Architecture

The least commonly used VPN architecture is the host-to-host model, which is typically used for special purpose needs, such as system administrators performing remote management of a single server. In this case, the organization configures the server to provide VPN services and the system administrators' hosts to act as VPN clients. The system administrators use the VPN client when needed to establish encrypted connections to the remote server. Figure 2-4 shows an example of an IPsec network architecture that uses the host-to-host model to provide a protected connection to a server for a user.

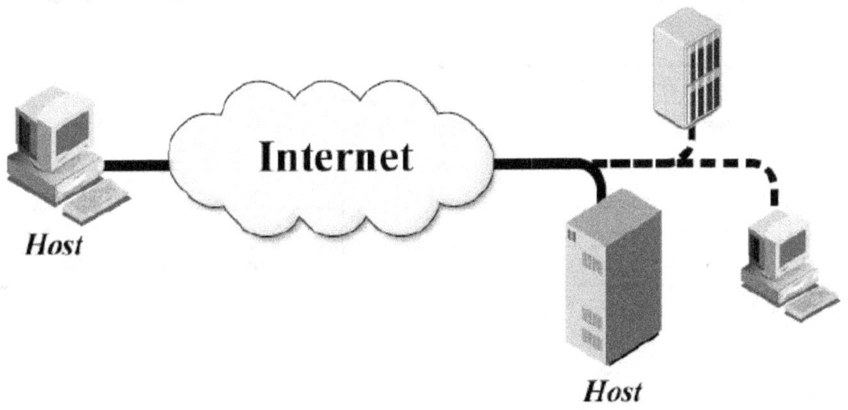

Figure 2-4. Host-to-Host Architecture Example

In this model, IPsec connections are created as needed for each individual VPN user. Users' hosts have been configured to act as IPsec clients with the IPsec server. When a user wishes to use resources on the IPsec server, the user's host initiates communications with the IPsec server. The user is asked by the IPsec server to authenticate before the connection can be established. The client and server exchange information, and if the authentication is successful, the IPsec connection is established. The user can now use the server, and the network traffic between the user's host and the server will be protected by the IPsec connection.

As shown in Figure 2-4, the host-to-host VPN is the only model that provides protection for data throughout its transit. This can be a problem, because network-based firewalls, intrusion detection systems, and other devices cannot be placed to inspect the decrypted data, which effectively circumvents certain layers of security.[13] The host-to-host model is most often used when a small number of trusted users need to use or administer a remote system that requires the use of insecure protocols (e.g., a legacy system) and can be updated to provide VPN services.

The host-to-host model is resource-intensive to implement and maintain in terms of user and host management. Host-to-host VPNs are not transparent to users because they must authenticate before using

---

12 Most (but not all) personal computer operating systems have built-in VPN clients, so it may be necessary to install VPN clients on some hosts.

13 Device placement can also be an issue in host-to-gateway and gateway-to-gateway architectures, but in those architectures it is usually possible to move devices or deploy additional devices to inspect decrypted data. This is not possible with a host-to-host architecture.

the VPN. Also, all user systems and servers that will participate in VPNs need to have VPN software installed and/or configured.

2.2.4 Model Comparison

Table 2-1 provides a brief comparison of the three VPN architecture models.

Table 2-1. Comparison of VPN Architecture Models

Feature	Gateway-to-gateway	Host-to-gateway	Host-to-host
Provides protection between client and local gateway	No	N/A (client is VPN endpoint)	N/A (client is VPN endpoint)
Provides protection between VPN endpoints	Yes	Yes	Yes
Provides protection between remote gateway and remote server (behind gateway)	No	No	N/A (server is VPN endpoint)
Transparent to users	Yes	No	No
Transparent to users' systems	Yes	No	No
Transparent to servers	Yes	Yes	No

2.3 Summary

Section 2 describes the TCP/IP model and its layers—application, transport, network, and data link—and explained how security controls at each layer provide different types of protection for TCP/IP communications. IPsec, a network layer security control, can provide several types of protection for data, depending on its configuration. Most IPsec implementations provide VPN services to protect communications between networks. The section describes VPNs and highlights the three primary VPN architecture models. The following summarizes the key points from Section 2:

- TCP/IP is widely used throughout the world to provide network communications. The TCP/IP model is composed of the following four layers, each having its own security controls that provide different types of protection:
  - **Application layer**, which sends and receives data for particular applications. Separate controls must be established for each application; this provides a very high degree of control and flexibility over each application's security, but it may be very resource-intensive. Creating new application layer security controls is also more likely to create vulnerabilities. Another potential issue is that some applications may not be capable of providing such protection or being modified to do so.
  - **Transport layer**, which provides connection-oriented or connectionless services for transporting application layer services across networks. Controls at this layer can protect the data in a single communications session between two hosts. The most frequently used transport layer control is TLS/SSL, which most often secures HTTP traffic. To be used, transport layer controls must be supported by both the clients and servers.

- **Network layer**, which routes packets across networks. Controls at this layer apply to all applications and are not application-specific, so applications do not have to be modified to use the controls. However, this provides less control and flexibility for protecting specific applications than transport and application layer controls. Network layer controls can protect both the data within packets and the IP information for each packet.

- **Data link layer**, which handles communications on the physical network components. Data link layer controls are suitable for protecting a specific physical link, such as a dedicated circuit between two buildings or a dial-up modem connection to an ISP. Because each physical link must be secured separately, data link layer controls generally are not feasible for protecting connections that involve several links, such as connections across the Internet.

■ IPsec is a framework of open standards for ensuring private communications over IP networks which has become the most commonly used network layer security control. It can provide several types of protection, including maintaining confidentiality and integrity, authenticating the origin of data, preventing packet replay and traffic analysis, and providing access protection.

■ A VPN is a virtual network built on top of existing networks that can provide a secure communications mechanism for data and IP information transmitted between networks. VPNs generally rely on both symmetric and asymmetric cryptography algorithms. Asymmetric cryptography is used to provide peer authentication; symmetric encryption is used to protect the actual data transfers because of its relative efficiency.

■ Although VPNs can reduce the risks of networking, they cannot eliminate it. For example, a VPN implementation may have flaws in algorithms or software that attackers can exploit. Also, VPN implementations often have at least a slightly negative impact on availability, because they add components and services to existing network infrastructures.

■ There are three primary models for VPN architectures, as follows:

  - **Gateway-to-gateway.** It connects two networks by deploying a gateway to each network and establishing a VPN connection between the two gateways. Communications between hosts on the two networks are then passed through the VPN connection, which provides protection for them. No protection is provided between each host and its local gateway. The gateway-to-gateway is most often used when connecting two secured networks, such as a branch office and headquarters, over the Internet. This often replaces more costly private WAN circuits. Gateway-to-gateway VPNs are typically transparent to users and do not involve installing or configuring any software on clients or servers.

  - **Host-to-gateway.** It connects hosts on various networks with hosts on the organization's network by deploying a gateway to the organization's network and permitting external hosts to establish individual VPN connections to that gateway. Communications are protected between the hosts and the gateway, but not between the gateway and the destination hosts within the organization. The host-to-gateway model is most often used when connecting hosts on unsecured networks to resources on secured networks, such as linking traveling employees to headquarters over the Internet. Host-to-gateway VPNs are typically not transparent to users because each user must authenticate before using the VPN and each host must have VPN client software installed and configured.

  - **Host-to-host.** It connects hosts to a single target host by deploying VPN software to each host and configuring the target host to receive VPN connections from the other hosts. This is the only VPN model that provides protection for data throughout its transit. It is most often used when a small number of users need to use or administer a remote system that requires the use of insecure protocols and can be updated to provide VPN services. The host-to-host model is resource-intensive to implement and maintain because it requires configuration on each host involved, including the target.

3. IPsec Fundamentals

IPsec is a collection of protocols that assist in protecting communications over IP networks.[14] IPsec protocols work together in various combinations to provide protection for communications. This section will focus on the three primary components—the Encapsulating Security Payload (ESP), Authentication Header (AH), and Internet Key Exchange (IKE) protocols—explaining the purpose and function of each protocol, and showing how they work together to create IPsec connections. Also, this section will discuss the value of using the IP Payload Compression Protocol (IPComp) as part of an IPsec implementation.

3.1 Authentication Header (AH)

AH,[15] one of the IPsec security protocols, provides integrity protection for packet headers and data, as well as user authentication. It can optionally provide replay protection and access protection. AH cannot encrypt any portion of packets. In the initial version of IPsec, the ESP protocol could provide only encryption, not authentication, so AH and ESP were often used together to provide both confidentiality and integrity protection for communications. Because authentication capabilities were added to ESP in the second version of IPsec, AH has become less significant; in fact, some IPsec software no longer supports AH. However, AH is still of value because AH can authenticate portions of packets that ESP cannot. Also, many existing IPsec implementations are using AH, so this guide includes a discussion of AH for completeness.[16]

3.1.1 AH Modes

AH has two modes: transport and tunnel. In *tunnel mode*, AH creates a new IP header for each packet; in *transport mode*, AH does not create a new IP header. In IPsec architectures that use a gateway, the true source or destination IP address for packets must be altered to be the gateway's IP address. Because transport mode cannot alter the original IP header or create a new IP header, transport mode is generally used in host-to-host architectures.[17] As shown in Figures 3-1 and 3-2, AH provides integrity protection for the entire packet, regardless of which mode is used. (As explained in Section 3.1.2, IP header fields that can change unpredictably while in transit are not integrity-protected.)

New IP Header	AH Header	Original IP Header	Transport and Application Protocol Headers and Data
Authenticated (Integrity Protection)			

Figure 3-1. AH Tunnel Mode Packet

IP Header	AH Header	Transport and Application Protocol Headers and Data
Authenticated (Integrity Protection)		

Figure 3-2. AH Transport Mode Packet

---

14 RFC 2401, *Security Architecture for the Internet Protocol*, provides an overview of IPsec. The RFC is available for download at http://www.ietf.org/rfc/rfc2401.txt.

15 AH is IP protocol number 51. The AH version 2 standard is defined in RFC 2402, *IP Authentication Header*, available at http://www.ietf.org/rfc/rfc2402.txt.

16 AH is also required by some protocols, such as Cellular IPv6. More information is available in RFC 3316, *Internet Protocol Version 6 (IPv6) for Some Second and Third Generation Cellular Hosts*, at http://www.ietf.org/rfc/rfc3316.txt.

17 RFC 3884, *Use of IPsec Transport Mode for Dynamic Routing*, proposes a way to use transport mode to provide tunnels via IP-in-IP. It is available at http://www.ietf.org/rfc/rfc3884.txt. More information on IP-in-IP is available from RFC 2003, *IP Encapsulation within IP*, available at http://www.ietf.org/rfc/rfc2003.txt.

3.1.2 Integrity Protection Process

The first step of integrity protection is to create a hash by using a keyed hash algorithm, also known as a message authentication code (MAC) algorithm. A standard hash algorithm generates a hash based on a message, while a *keyed hash algorithm* creates a hash based on both a message and a secret key shared by the two endpoints. The hash is added to the packet, and the packet is sent to the recipient. The recipient can then regenerate the hash using the shared key and confirm that the two hashes match, which provides integrity protection for the packet. IPsec uses hash message authentication code (HMAC) algorithms,[18] which perform two keyed hashes. Examples of keyed hash algorithms are HMAC-MD5 and HMAC-SHA-1.[19] Another common MAC algorithm is AES Cipher Block Chaining MAC (AES-XCBC-MAC-96).[20]

Technically, Figures 3-1 and 3-2 are somewhat misleading because it is not possible to protect the integrity of the entire IP header. Certain IP header fields, such as time to live (TTL) and the IP header checksum, are dynamic and may change during routine communications. If the hash is calculated on all the original IP header values, and some of those values legitimately change in transit, the recalculated hash will be different. The destination would conclude that the packet had changed in transit and that its integrity had been violated. To avoid this problem, IP header fields that may legitimately change in transit in an unpredictable manner are excluded from the integrity protection calculations.

This same principle explains why AH is often incompatible with network address translation (NAT) implementations. The IP source and destination address fields are included in the AH integrity protection calculations. If these addresses are altered by a NAT device (e.g., changing the source address from a private to a public address), the AH integrity protection calculation made by the destination will not match. (Section 4.2.1 contains information on techniques for overcoming NAT-related issues.)

3.1.3 AH Header

AH adds a header to each packet. As shown in Figure 3-3, each AH header is composed of six fields:

- **Next Header.** This field contains the IP protocol number for the next packet payload. In tunnel mode, the payload is an IP packet, so the Next Header value is set to 4 for IP-in-IP. In transport mode, the payload is usually a transport-layer protocol, often TCP (protocol number 6) or UDP (protocol number 17).
- **Payload Length.** This field contains the length of the payload in 4-byte increments, minus 2.
- **Reserved.** This value is reserved for future use, so it should be set to 0.
- **Security Parameters Index (SPI).**[21] Each endpoint of each IPsec connection has an arbitrarily chosen SPI value, which acts as a unique identifier for the connection. The recipient uses the SPI value, along with the destination IP address and (optionally) the IPsec protocol type (in this case, AH), to determine which Security Association (SA) is being used. This tells the recipient which

---

18 For more information on HMAC, see RFC 2104, *HMAC: Keyed-Hashing for Message Authentication* (http://www.ietf.org/rfc/rfc2104.txt).

19 Federal agencies are required to use FIPS-approved algorithms and FIPS-validated cryptographic modules. HMAC-SHA-1 is a FIPS-approved algorithm, but HMAC-MD5 is not.

20 For more information on AES-XCBC-MAC-96, see RFC 3566, *The AES-XCBC-MAC-96 Algorithm and Its Use with IPsec*, available at http://www.ietf.org/rfc/rfc3566.txt. AES-XCBC-MAC-96 is not a FIPS-approved algorithm.

21 SPI is sometimes known as Security Parameter Index instead of Security Parameters Index. RFC 2402, *IP Authentication Header*, and RFC 2406, *IP Encapsulating Security Payload (ESP)*, use the word Parameters; RFC 2401, *Security Architecture for the Internet Protocol*, uses Parameter,

IPsec protocols and algorithms have been applied to the packet. More details about SAs can be found in Section 3.3.

- **Sequence Number.** Each packet is assigned a sequential sequence number, and only packets within a sliding window of sequence numbers are accepted. This provides protection against replay attacks because duplicate packets will use the same sequence number. This also helps to thwart denial of service attacks because old packets that are replayed will have sequence numbers outside the window, and will be dropped immediately without performing any more processing.

- **Authentication Information.** This field contains the MAC output described in Section 3.1.2. The recipient of the packet can recalculate the MAC to confirm that the packet has not been altered in transit.

Next Header	Payload Length	Reserved
Security Parameters Index		
Sequence Number		
Authentication Information		

Figure 3-3. AH Header

3.1.4 How AH Works

The best way to understand how AH works is by reviewing and analyzing actual AH packets. Figure 3-4 shows the bytes that compose an actual AH packet. The values on the left side are the packet bytes in hex, and the values on the right side are attempted ASCII translations of each hex byte. (Bytes that cannot be translated into a printable ASCII character are represented by a dot.) Figure 3-4 indicates each section of the AH packet: Ethernet header, IP header, AH header, and payload.[22] Based on the fields shown in Figures 3-1 and 3-2, this is a transport mode packet because it only contains a single IP header. In this case, the payload contains an ICMP echo request—a ping. The original ping contained alphabetic sequences, represented in the packet by ascending hex values (e.g., 61, 62, 63). After AH was applied, the ICMP payload is unaffected. This is because AH only provides integrity protection, not encryption.

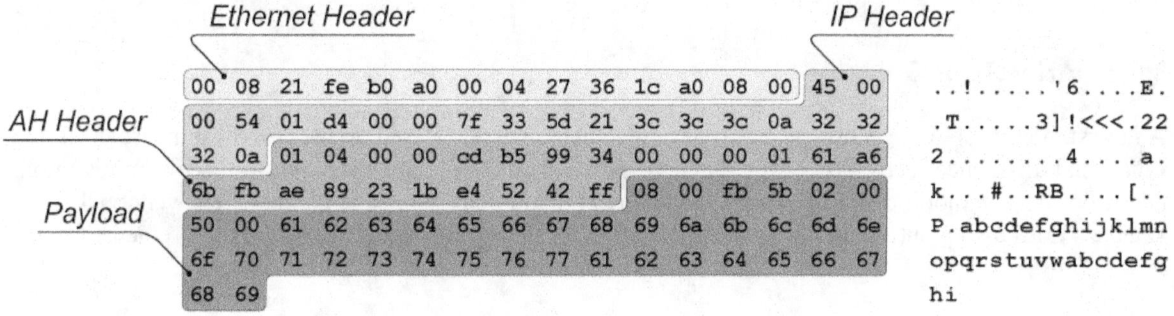

Figure 3-4. Sample AH Transport Mode Packet

22 This view of the packet was produced by Ethereal, a free utility that can capture packets and analyze them according to various protocols. It is available from http://www.ethereal.com/.

Figure 3-5 shows the AH header fields from the first four packets in an AH session between hosts A and B. The fields in the first header have been labeled, and they correspond to the fields identified in Figure 3-3. Items of interest are as follows:

- **SPI.** Host A uses the hex value cdb59934 for the SPI in both its packets, while host B uses the hex value a6b32c00 for the SPI in both packets. This reflects that an AH connection is actually composed of two one-way connections, each with its own SPI.
- **Sequence Number.** Both hosts initially set the sequence number to 1, and both incremented the number to 2 for their second packets.
- **Authentication Information.** The authentication (integrity protection) information, which is a keyed hash based on virtually all the bytes in the packet, is different in each packet. This value should be different even if only one byte in a hashed section of the packet changes.

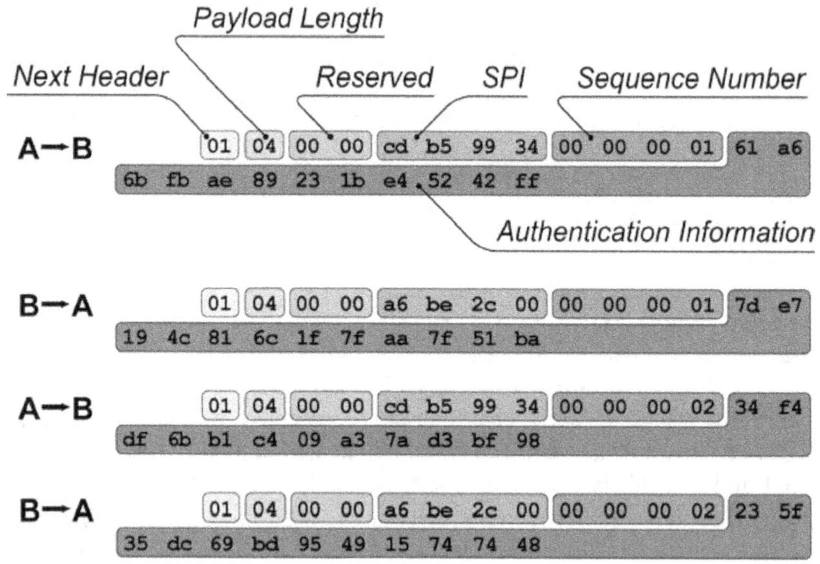

Figure 3-5. AH Header Fields from Sample Packet

3.1.5 AH Version 3

A new standard for AH, version 3, is currently in development.[23] Based on the current standard draft, the functional differences between version 2 and version 3 should be relatively minor to IPsec administrators and users—some modifications to the SPI, and an optional longer sequence number. The version 3 standard draft also points to another standard draft that lists cryptographic algorithm requirements for

[23] The current draft of the proposed standard for AH version 3 is available at http://www.ietf.org/internet-drafts/draft-ietf-ipsec-rfc2402bis-xx.txt. There is also a new proposed standard to replace RFC 2401, which provides an overview of IPsec version 2 (which includes AH version 2 and ESP version 2). The current version of the replacement for RFC 2401 is available at http://www.ietf.org/internet-drafts/draft-ietf-ipsec-rfc2401bis-xx.txt.

AH.[24] The draft mandates support for HMAC-SHA1-96, strongly recommends support for AES-XCBC-MAC-96, and also recommends support for HMAC-MD5-96.

3.1.6 AH Summary

- AH provides integrity protection for all packet headers and data, with the exception of a few IP header fields that routinely change in transit.
- Because AH includes source and destination IP addresses in its integrity protection calculations, AH is often incompatible with NAT. Section 4 describes techniques for overcoming this.
- Currently, most IPsec implementations support the second version of IPsec, in which ESP can provide integrity protection services through authentication. The use of AH has significantly declined. In fact, some IPsec implementations no longer support AH.
- AH still provides one benefit that ESP does not: integrity protection for the outermost IP header.[25]

3.2 Encapsulating Security Payload (ESP)

ESP[26] is the second core IPsec security protocol. In the initial version of IPsec, ESP provided only encryption for packet payload data. Integrity protection was provided by the AH protocol if needed, as discussed in Section 3.1. In the second version of IPsec, ESP became more flexible. It can perform authentication to provide integrity protection, although not for the outermost IP header. Also, ESP's encryption can be disabled through the Null ESP Encryption Algorithm. Therefore, in all but the oldest IPsec implementations, ESP can be used to provide only encryption; encryption and integrity protection; or only integrity protection.[27] This section mainly addresses the features and characteristics of the second version of ESP; the third version, currently in development, is described near the end of the section.

3.2.1 ESP Modes

ESP has two modes: transport and tunnel. In *tunnel mode*, ESP creates a new IP header for each packet. The new IP header lists the endpoints of the ESP tunnel (such as two IPsec gateways) as the source and destination of the packet. Because of this, tunnel mode can be used with all three VPN architecture models described in Section 2. As shown in Figure 3-6, tunnel mode can encrypt and/or protect the integrity of both the data and the original IP header for each packet.[28] Encrypting the data protects it from being accessed or modified by unauthorized parties; encrypting the IP header conceals the nature of the communications, such as the actual source or destination of the packet. If authentication is being used for integrity protection, each packet will have an ESP Authentication section after the ESP trailer.

---

24 The current draft of the proposed standard for ESP and AH cryptographic algorithms is available at http://www.ietf.org/internet-drafts/draft-ietf-ipsec-esp-ah-algorithms-xx.txt.

25 Using IKE to negotiate IPsec protections can indirectly provide authentication for the source and destination IP addresses of ESP-protected packets as well.

26 ESP is IP protocol number 50. The ESP version 2 standard is defined in RFC 2406, *IP Encapsulating Security Payload (ESP)*, available at http://www.ietf.org/rfc/rfc2406.txt.

27 As specified in RFC 2406, ESP version 2 is only required to support DES for encryption, but most implementations support stronger encryption algorithms. NIST recommends that AH or ESP integrity protection should be used whenever ESP encryption is used. Research has shown that IPsec is susceptible to multiple types of attacks if ESP encryption is used without AH or ESP integrity protection. For more information on such attacks, see the paper titled *Problem Areas for the IP Security Protocols* by Steven Bellovin, available at http://www.research.att.com/~smb/papers/badesp.pdf.

28 Either ESP encryption or ESP authentication (but not both) can be set to null, disabling that capability.

New IP Header	ESP Header	Original IP Header	Transport and Application Protocol Headers and Data	ESP Trailer	ESP Authentication (optional)
		Encrypted			
	Authenticated (Integrity Protection)				

Figure 3-6. ESP Tunnel Mode Packet

ESP tunnel mode is used far more frequently than ESP transport mode. In *transport mode*, ESP uses the original IP header instead of creating a new one. Figure 3-7 shows that in transport mode, ESP can only encrypt and/or protect the integrity of packet payloads and certain ESP components, but not IP headers. As with AH, ESP transport mode is generally only used in host-to-host architectures. Also, transport mode is incompatible with NAT. For example, in each TCP packet, the TCP checksum is calculated on both TCP and IP fields, including the source and destination addresses in the IP header. If NAT is being used, one or both of the IP addresses are altered, so NAT needs to recalculate the TCP checksum. If ESP is encrypting packets, the TCP header is encrypted; NAT cannot recalculate the checksum, so NAT fails. This is not an issue in tunnel mode; because the entire TCP packet is hidden, NAT will not attempt to recalculate the TCP checksum. However, tunnel mode and NAT have other potential compatibility issues.[29] Section 4.2.1 provides guidance on overcoming NAT-related issues.

IP Header	ESP Header	Transport and Application Protocol Headers and Data	ESP Trailer	ESP Authentication – optional
		Encrypted		
	Authenticated (Integrity Protection)			

Figure 3-7. ESP Transport Mode Packet

3.2.2 Encryption Process

As described in Section 3.2, ESP uses symmetric cryptography to provide encryption for IPsec packets. Accordingly, both endpoints of an IPsec connection protected by ESP encryption must use the same key to encrypt and decrypt the packets. When an endpoint encrypts data, it divides the data into small blocks (for the AES algorithm, 128 bits each), and then performs multiple sets of cryptographic operations (known as *rounds*) using the data blocks and key. Encryption algorithms that work in this way are known as *block cipher algorithms*. When the other endpoint receives the encrypted data, it performs decryption using the same key and a similar process, but with the steps reversed and the cryptographic operations altered. Examples of encryption algorithms used by ESP are AES-Cipher Block Chaining (AES-CBC), AES Counter Mode (AES-CTR), and Triple DES (3DES).[30]

---

29 One possible issue is the inability to perform incoming source address validation to confirm that the source address is the same as that under which the IKE SA was negotiated. Other possible issues include packet fragmentation, NAT mapping timeouts, and multiple clients behind the same NAT device.

30 For a detailed explanation of how AES encryption works, see FIPS 197, *Advanced Encryption Standard (AES)*, available at http://csrc.nist.gov/publications/fips/fips197/fips-197.pdf.

3.2.3 ESP Packet Fields

ESP adds a header and a trailer around each packet's payload. As shown in Figure 3-8, each ESP header is composed of two fields:

- **SPI.** Each endpoint of each IPsec connection has an arbitrarily chosen SPI value, which acts as a unique identifier for the connection. The recipient uses the SPI value, along with the destination IP address and (optionally) the IPsec protocol type (in this case, ESP), to determine which SA is being used.
- **Sequence Number.** Each packet is assigned a sequential sequence number, and only packets within a sliding window of sequence numbers are accepted. This provides protection against replay attacks because duplicate packets will use the same sequence number. This also helps to thwart denial of service attacks because old packets that are replayed will have sequence numbers outside the window, and will be dropped immediately without performing any more processing.

The next part of the packet is the payload. It is composed of the payload data, which is encrypted, and the initialization vector (IV), which is not encrypted. The IV is used during encryption. Its value is different in every packet, so if two packets have the same content, the inclusion of the IV will cause the encryption of the two packets to have different results. This makes ESP less susceptible to cryptanalysis.

The third part of the packet is the ESP trailer, which contains at least two fields and may optionally include one more:

- **Padding.** An ESP packet may optionally contain *padding*, which is additional bytes of data that make the packet larger and are discarded by the packet's recipient. Because ESP uses block ciphers for encryption, padding may be needed so that the encrypted data is an integral multiple of the block size. Padding may also be needed to ensure that the ESP trailer ends on a multiple of 4 bytes. Additional padding may also be used to alter the size of each packet, concealing how many bytes of actual data the packet contains. This is helpful in deterring traffic analysis.
- **Padding Length.** This number indicates how many bytes long the padding is. The Padding Length field is mandatory.
- **Next Header.** In tunnel mode, the payload is an IP packet, so the Next Header value is set to 4 for IP-in-IP. In transport mode, the payload is usually a transport-layer protocol, often TCP (protocol number 6) or UDP (protocol number 17). Every ESP trailer contains a Next Header value.

If ESP integrity protection is enabled, the ESP trailer is followed by an Authentication Information field. Like AH, the field contains the MAC output described in Section 3.1.2. Unlike AH, the MAC in ESP does not include the outermost IP header in its calculations. The recipient of the packet can recalculate the MAC to confirm that the portions of the packet other than the outermost IP header have not been altered in transit.

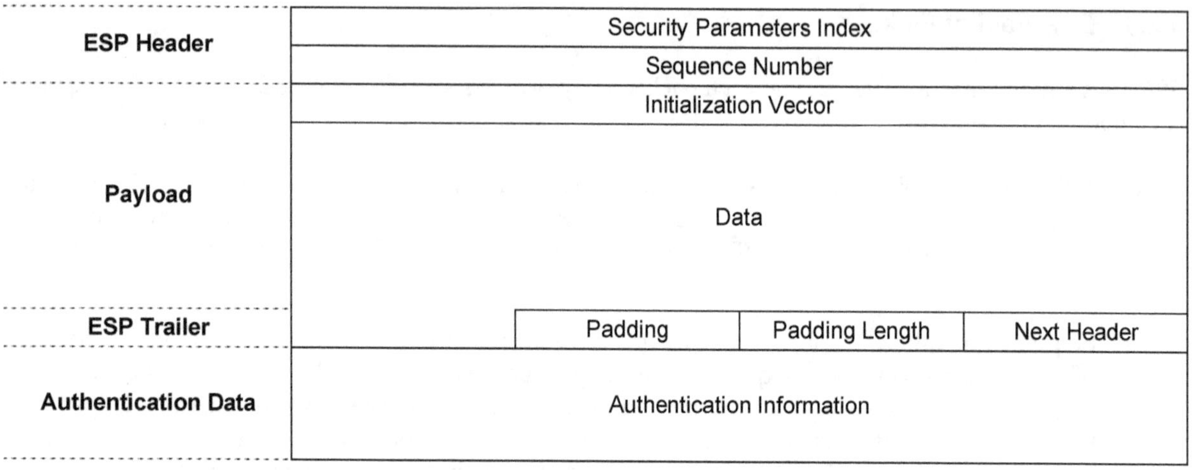

Figure 3-8. ESP Packet Fields

3.2.4 How ESP Works

Reviewing and analyzing actual ESP packets can provide a better understanding of how ESP works, particularly when compared with AH packets. Figure 3-9 shows the bytes that compose an actual ESP packet and their ASCII representations, in the same format used in Section 3.1.4. The alphabetic sequence that was visible in the AH-protected payload cannot be seen in the ESP-protected payload because it has been encrypted. The ESP packet only contains five sections: Ethernet header, IP header, ESP header, encrypted data (payload and ESP trailer), and (optionally) authentication information. From the encrypted data, it is not possible to determine if this packet was generated in transport mode or tunnel mode. However, because the IP header is unencrypted, the IP protocol field in the header does reveal which protocol the payload uses (in this case, ESP). As shown in Figures 3-6 and 3-7, the unencrypted fields in both modes (tunnel and transport) are the same.

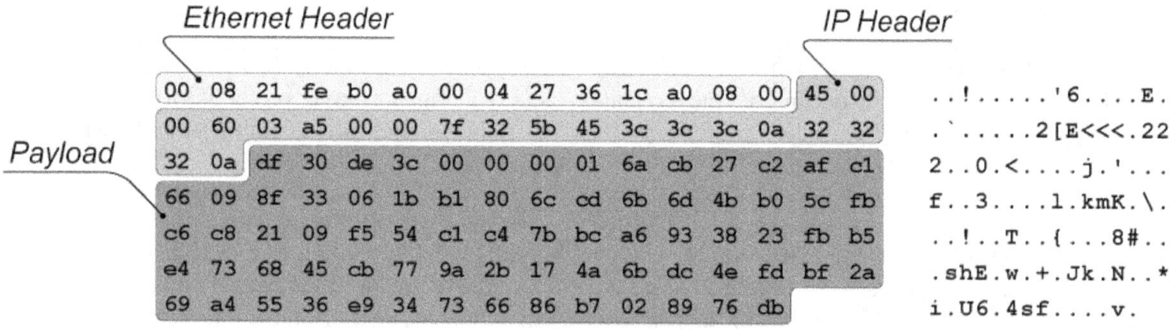

Figure 3-9. ESP Packet Capture

Although it is difficult to tell from Figure 3-9, the ESP header fields are not encrypted. Figure 3-10 shows the ESP header fields from the first four packets in an ESP session between hosts A and B. The SPI and Sequence Number fields work the same way in ESP that they do in AH. Each host uses a different static SPI value for its packets, which corresponds to an ESP connection being composed of two one-way connections, each with its own SPI. Also, both hosts initially set the sequence number to 1, and both incremented the number to 2 for their second packets.

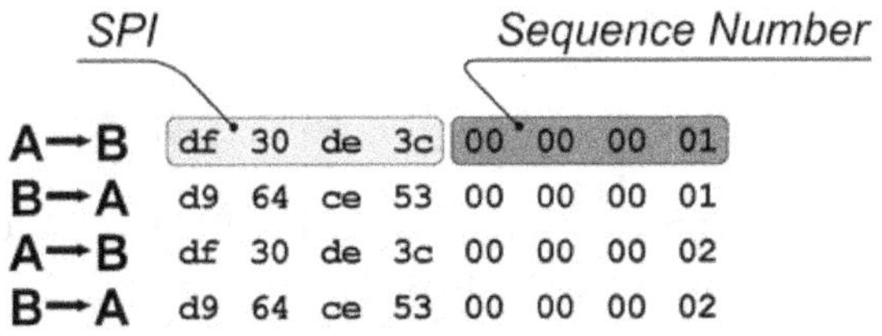

Figure 3-10. ESP Header Fields from Sample Packets

3.2.5 ESP Version 3

A new standard for ESP, version 3, is currently in development.[31] Based on the current standard draft, there should be several major functional differences between version 2 and version 3, including the following:

- The standard for ESP version 2 required ESP implementations to support using ESP encryption only (without integrity protection). The proposed ESP version 3 standard makes support for this optional.
- ESP can use an optional longer sequence number, just like the proposed AH version 3 standard.
- ESP version 3 supports the use of combined mode algorithms (e.g., AES Counter with CBC-MAC [AES-CCM]).[32] Rather than using separate algorithms for encryption and integrity protection, a combined mode algorithm provides both encryption and integrity protection.

The version 3 standard draft also points to another standard draft that lists encryption and integrity protection cryptographic algorithm requirements for ESP.[33] For encryption algorithms, the draft mandates support for the null encryption algorithm and 3DES-CBC, strongly recommends support for AES-CBC (with 128-bit keys), recommends support for AES-CTR, and discourages support for DES-CBC.[34] For integrity protection algorithms, the draft mandates support for HMAC-SHA1-96 and the null authentication algorithm, strongly recommends support for AES-XCBC-MAC-96, and also recommends support for HMAC-MD5-96. The standard draft does not recommend any combined mode algorithms.

3.2.6 ESP Summary

- In tunnel mode, ESP can provide encryption and integrity protection for an encapsulated IP packet, as well as authentication of the ESP header. Tunnel mode can be compatible with NAT. However, protocols with embedded addresses (e.g., FTP, IRC, SIP) can present additional complications.

---

31 The current draft of the proposed standard for ESP version 3 is available at http://www.ietf.org/internet-drafts/draft-ietf-ipsec-esp-v3-xx.txt.

32 More information on AES-CCM can be found in the Internet-Draft *Using AES CCM Mode With IPsec ESP* at http://www.ietf.org/internet-drafts/draft-ietf-ipsec-ciph-aes-ccm-xx.txt.

33 The current draft of the proposed standard for ESP and AH cryptographic algorithms is available at http://www.ietf.org/internet-drafts/draft-ietf-ipsec-esp-ah-algorithms-xx.txt.

34 More information on AES-CTR is available from RFC 3686, *Using Advanced Encryption Standard (AES) Counter Mode With IPsec Encapsulating Security Payload (ESP)*, at http://www.ietf.org/rfc/rfc3686.txt.

- In transport mode, ESP can provide encryption and integrity protection for the payload of an IP packet, as well as integrity protection for the ESP header. Transport mode is not compatible with NAT.
- ESP tunnel mode is the most commonly used IPsec mode. Because it can encrypt the original IP header, it can conceal the true source and destination of the packet. Also, ESP can add padding to packets, further complicating attempts to perform traffic analysis.
- Although ESP can be used to provide encryption or integrity protection (or both), ESP encryption should not be used without integrity protection.

3.3 Internet Key Exchange (IKE)

The purpose of the Internet Key Exchange (IKE) protocol is to negotiate, create, and manage security associations.[35] *Security association* (SA) is a generic term for a set of values that define the IPsec features and protections applied to a connection. SAs can also be manually created, using values agreed upon in advance by both parties, but these SAs cannot be updated; this method does not scale for real-life large-scale VPNs. IKE uses five different types of exchanges to create security associations, transfer status and error information, and define new Diffie-Hellman groups. In IPsec, IKE is used to provide a secure mechanism for establishing IPsec-protected connections. The following sections describe the five types of IKE exchanges (main mode, aggressive mode, quick mode, informational, and group) and explain how they work together for IPsec. This section also briefly discusses IKE version 2 and how it differs from the original IKE protocol.

3.3.1 Phase One Exchange

The purpose of the IKE phase one exchange is for the two IPsec endpoints to successfully negotiate a secure channel through which an IPsec SA can be negotiated. The secure channel created during phase one is commonly known as an *IKE SA*. The purpose of the IKE SA is to provide bidirectional encryption and authentication for other IKE exchanges: the negotiations that comprise phase two, the transfer of status and error information, and the creation of additional Diffie-Hellman groups. In fact, a phase one IKE exchange must be successfully completed before any of the other IKE exchange types can be performed. An IKE SA can be established through one of two modes: main mode and aggressive mode.

3.3.1.1 Main mode

Main mode negotiates the establishment of the IKE SA through three pairs of messages. In the first pair of messages, each endpoint proposes parameters to be used for the SA.[36] Four of the parameters are mandatory, and are collectively referred to as the *protection suite*:

- **Encryption Algorithm.** This specifies the algorithm to be used to encrypt data. Examples of encryption algorithms are DES, 3DES, CAST, RC5, IDEA, Blowfish, and AES. Section 4.2.3 provides guidance on selecting an encryption algorithm.

---

35 The IKE standard is defined in RFC 2409, *The Internet Key Exchange (IKE)*, available at http://www.ietf.org/rfc/rfc2409.txt. By default, IKE uses UDP port 500 for its communications. Section 4.2.1.1 describes NAT Traversal, which moves IKE communications to UDP port 4500.

36 The connection initiator could propose several values for various parameters and allow the other endpoint to select from those values. Because there are so many possible combinations of parameters, it is recommended to use common parameter combinations or to configure the endpoints to use the same parameters in advance. This supports the interoperability of the endpoints.

- **Integrity Protection Algorithm.** This indicates which keyed hash algorithm should be used for integrity protection. As described in Section 3.1.2, HMAC-MD5 and HMAC-SHA-1 are commonly used keyed hash algorithms. Section 4.2.3 provides information on choosing an integrity protection algorithm.

- **Authentication Method.** There are several possible methods for authenticating the two endpoints to each other, including the following:

  - **Pre-shared Keys.** Each endpoint has been given the same secret key in advance. The endpoints use the key to generate a value that is then used to create the secret keys that will be used to protect the phase 1 secure channel, as well as the eventual IPsec SA. Successful completion of the phase 1 IKE negotiation constitutes proof that each peer possesses the pre-shared secret key, which serves to authenticate the peers to each other.

  - **Digital Signatures.** Each endpoint has its own digital certificate that contains a public key. The endpoint uses the corresponding private key to digitally sign data before sending it to the other endpoint, which verifies the signature using the peer's public key. The digital signature algorithm choices are RSA and the Digital Signature Standard (DSS).

  - **Public Key Encryption.** Instead of using the public/private key pair for signing data, each peer encrypts data with its own private key and decrypts data with the peer's public key. The algorithm typically used for public key encryption is RSA. Public key encryption-based authentication typically relies upon the establishment of a public key infrastructure (PKI) implementation and the issuance of digital certificates. This authentication method is defined in the IKE standard, but it is not commonly implemented or used.

  - **External Authentication.** Although not specified by the current IKE standard, some IPsec implementations support the use of external authentication servers and services[37] such as Kerberos v5. In the Kerberos method, a Kerberos server maintains all of the keys for all devices within its domain. Kerberos may also be used to authenticate the hosts; however, the identity of the endpoints will not be concealed until the third set of messages, as described later in this section. (When some authentication methods are used, such as pre-shared keys or digital signatures, the identity of the endpoints is protected during all three sets of messages.)

- **Diffie-Hellman (DH) Group.** Diffie-Hellman is used to generate a shared secret for the endpoints in a secure manner, so that an observer of the IKE phase one exchange cannot determine the shared secret.[38] This shared secret is then used to generate a value that is used as input to the calculations for the phase 1 and 2 secret keys. As shown in Table 3-1, each DH group number corresponds to a key length and an encryption generator type (exponentiation over a prime modulus [MODP] or elliptic curve over $G[2^N]$, also known as EC2N).[39] Although groups using elliptic curves may be more efficient than prime modulus groups, elliptic curve groups are not generally used because of intellectual property concerns involving the licensing of elliptic curve cryptography algorithms.

---

37 Section 3.3.5 describes the Extensible Authentication Protocol (EAP), which permits IPsec to use external authentication services such as Kerberos and Remote Authentication Dial In User Service (RADIUS). EAP is supported in the proposed standard for the second version of IKE.

38 This is not the same as the pre-shared key described earlier in the section.

39 RFC 2409 defines groups 1 through 4. RFC 3526, *More Modular Exponential (MODP) Diffie-Hellman Groups for Internet Key Exchange (IKE)*, defines the other groups shown in the table. RFC 2409 requires IKE implementations to support Group 1 and recommends that they also support Group 2. Support for other groups is also acceptable. Section 3.3.4 explains how IKE can use customized Diffie-Hellman groups.

Table 3-1. Diffie-Hellman Group Definitions

Group Number	Generator	Modulus or Field Size
1	MODP	768-bit modulus
2	MODP	1024-bit modulus
3	EC2N	155-bit field size
4	EC2N	185-bit field size
5	MODP	1536-bit modulus
14	MODP	2048-bit modulus
15	MODP	3072-bit modulus
16	MODP	4096-bit modulus
17	MODP	6144-bit modulus
18	MODP	8192-bit modulus

Besides negotiating the parameters of the IKE protection suite, the first pair of main mode messages also includes the exchange of cookies. The cookies are based partially on the other host's IP address and a time-based counter. This provides some protection against denial of service attacks because it occurs before the cryptographically-intensive operations in subsequent steps. Figure 3-11 shows Ethereal's interpretation of the initial message in the first pair of main mode messages. (Both messages in the pair contain the same fields, so the second message in the pair is omitted for brevity.) Besides the initial cookie value, Figure 3-11 shows many other items of interest, including which mode is being used (in this case, main mode); which encryption and hash algorithms should be used; and which authentication method should be used (in this case, pre-shared keys).[40]

[40] Figure 3-11 and other figures in this section refer to the Internet Security Association and Key Management Protocol (ISAKMP). As defined in RFC 2409, ISAKMP is a "framework for authentication and key exchange", and IKE is a specific implementation of the ISAKMP framework.

```
User Datagram Protocol, Src Port: isakmp (500), Dst Port: isakmp (500)
Internet Security Association and Key Management Protocol
    Initiator cookie: 0x04874D4D109ECCF4
    Responder cookie: 0x0000000000000000
    Next payload: Security Association (1)
    Version: 1.0
    Exchange type: Identity Protection (Main Mode) (2)
    Flags
        .... ...0 = No encryption
        .... ..0. = No commit
        .... .0.. = No authentication
    Message ID: 0x00000000
    Length: 84
    Security Association payload
        Next payload: NONE (0)
        Length: 56
        Domain of interpretation: IPSEC (1)
        Situation: IDENTITY (1)
        Proposal payload # 1
            Next payload: NONE (0)
            Length: 44
            Proposal number: 1
            Protocol ID: ISAKMP (1)
            SPI size: 0
            Number of transforms: 1
            Transform payload # 1
                Next payload: NONE (0)
                Length: 36
                Transform number: 1
                Transform ID: KEY_IKE (1)
                Encryption-Algorithm (1): DES-CBC (1)
                Hash-Algorithm (2): MD5 (1)
                Group-Description (4): Default 768-bit MODP group (1)
                Authentication-Method (3): PSK (1)
                Life-Type (11): Seconds (1)
                Life-Duration (12): Duration-Value (28800)
```

Figure 3-11. Ethereal Interpretation of a First Pair Main Mode Message

The second pair of main mode messages performs a key exchange through Diffie-Hellman, using the parameters negotiated during the first step. Figure 3-12 shows Ethereal's interpretation of the initial message in the second pair of main mode messages. (Both messages in the pair contain the same fields, so the second message in the pair is omitted for brevity.) Most of the packet is composed of the key exchange data, as well as a nonce.[41] The contents of the second pair of messages vary somewhat based on authentication method. Messages involving pre-shared key or digital signature-based authentication have the same fields—header, key, and nonce. Messages involving public key encryption-based authentication encrypt the nonce with the other endpoint's public key and exchange IDs (also protected by public keys). When pre-shared key or digital signature-based authentication is used, IDs are not exchanged until the third pair of messages so that the keys established through the Diffie-Hellman exchange can protect the IDs.

[41] A *nonce* is a non-repeating value that is used as input to several types of cryptographic calculations, including supporting the integrity of the negotiation. For example, host A sends a nonce to host B. Host B performs calculations and sends the results to host A; host A then uses the original nonce value to validate the results from host B. Nonces are also used to guarantee that each exchange is new, rather than a replay of a previous IKE exchange.

```
User Datagram Protocol, Src Port: isakmp (500), Dst Port: isakmp (500)
Internet Security Association and Key Management Protocol
    Initiator cookie: 0x04874D4D109ECCF4
    Responder cookie: 0x38945FD052E53D60
    Next payload: Key Exchange (4)
    Version: 1.0
    Exchange type: Identity Protection (Main Mode) (2)
    Flags
        .... ...0 = No encryption
        .... ..0. = No commit
        .... .0.. = No authentication
    Message ID: 0x00000000
    Length: 152
    Key Exchange payload
        Next payload: Nonce (10)
        Length: 100
        Key Exchange Data
    Nonce payload
        Next payload: NONE (0)
        Length: 24
        Nonce Data
```

Figure 3-12. Ethereal Interpretation of a Second Pair Main Mode Message

In the third pair of messages, each endpoint is authenticated to the other. Again, this depends on the negotiated authentication method. If preshared keys are specified, authenticating hash digests are exchanged; if digital signatures are specified, they are used. Regardless of the method in use, these messages are encrypted based on the information exchanged in the second pair of messages. Figure 3-13 shows Ethereal's interpretation of the initial message in the third pair of main mode messages. Other than the IKE header fields, the rest of the data is shown as encrypted.

```
User Datagram Protocol, Src Port: isakmp (500), Dst Port: isakmp (500)
Internet Security Association and Key Management Protocol
    Initiator cookie: 0x04874D4D109ECCF4
    Responder cookie: 0x38945FD052E53D60
    Next payload: Identification (5)
    Version: 1.0
    Exchange type: Identity Protection (Main Mode) (2)
    Flags
        .... ...1 = Encryption
        .... ..0. = No commit
        .... .0.. = No authentication
    Message ID: 0x00000000
    Length: 60
    Encrypted payload (32 bytes)
```

Figure 3-13. Ethereal Interpretation of a Third Pair Main Mode Message

Any of the pairs of main mode messages might also contain a vendor ID, which is a value that indicates the vendor of the sender's IPsec software. The vendor ID can be used to identify some of the sender's characteristics and preferences. For example, Section 4.2.1 describes the use of the vendor ID in overcoming NAT-related issues.

To summarize, main mode uses three pairs of messages. Each of the three pairs of messages has a different purpose. The first pair of messages negotiates the IKE SA parameters, the second pair performs a key exchange, and the third pair authenticates the endpoints to each other.

3.3.1.2 Aggressive mode

Aggressive mode offers a faster alternative to main mode. It negotiates the establishment of the IKE SA through three messages instead of three pairs of messages. The first two messages negotiate the IKE SA parameters and perform a key exchange; the second and third messages authenticate the endpoints to each other. The following provides more detail on each message:

- In the first message, endpoint A sends all the protection suite parameters, as well as its portion of the Diffie-Hellman key exchange, a nonce, and its identity.
- In the second message, endpoint B sends the protection suite parameters, its portion of the Diffie-Hellman key exchange, a nonce, its identity, and its authentication payload (through digital signature or hash).
- In the third message, endpoint A sends its authentication payload.

Aggressive mode negotiates all the same parameters as main mode through fewer messages. Also, unlike main mode, aggressive mode can be used with pre-shared secret key authentication for hosts without fixed IP addresses. However, with the increased speed of aggressive mode comes decreased security. Since the Diffie-Hellman key exchange begins in the first packet, the two parties do not have an opportunity to negotiate the Diffie-Hellman parameters. Also, the identity information is not always hidden in aggressive mode, so an observer could determine which parties were performing the negotiation. (Aggressive mode can conceal identity information in some cases when public keys have already been exchanged.) Aggressive mode negotiations are also susceptible to pre-shared key cracking, which can allow user impersonation and man-in-the-middle attacks.[42] Another potential issue is that while all IPsec devices must support main mode, aggressive mode support is optional. Unless there are performance issues, it is generally recommended to use main mode for the phase one exchange.[43]

3.3.2 Phase Two Exchange

The purpose of phase two is to establish an SA for the actual IPsec connection. This SA is referred to as the *IPsec SA*. Unlike IKE SA's, which are bidirectional, IPsec SA's are unidirectional. This means that an IPsec connection between two systems requires two security associations. The pair of IPsec SAs is created through a single mode, *quick mode*. Quick mode uses three messages to establish the SA. Remember that quick mode communications are encrypted by the method specified in the IKE SA created by phase one.

Figure 3-14 shows an Ethereal interpretation of a quick mode message. Although certain fields are visible (e.g., cookies, message ID, flags), most of the content of the message is encrypted. The following items list the most significant contents of the encrypted portion of the quick mode messages:

[42] For more information on the pre-shared key cracking issue, see the paper *PSK Cracking Using IKE Aggressive Mode* by Michael Thumann and Enno Rey. The paper is available at http://www.ernw.de/download/pskattack.pdf.

[43] Aggressive mode may also be needed if other requirements are forcing the use of preshared key authentication for peers without fixed addresses.

- In the first message, endpoint A sends keys, nonces, and IPsec SA parameter suggestions.[44] The nonces are an anti-replay measure.
- In the second message, endpoint B sends keys, nonces, and IPsec SA parameter selections, plus a hash for authentication.
- In the third message, endpoint A sends a hash for authentication.

```
User Datagram Protocol, Src Port: isakmp (500), Dst Port: isakmp (500)
Internet Security Association and Key Management Protocol
    Initiator cookie: 0x04874D4D109ECCF4
    Responder cookie: 0x38945FD052E53D60
    Next payload: Hash (8)
    Version: 1.0
    Exchange type: Quick Mode (32)
    Flags
        .... ...1 = Encryption
        .... ..0. = No commit
        .... .0.. = No authentication
    Message ID: 0x7DEA6802
    Length: 164
    Encrypted payload (136 bytes)
```

Figure 3-14. Ethereal Interpretation of a Quick Mode Message

After endpoint B validates the third message, the IPsec SAs are established. All active SAs are stored in a Security Association Database (SAD).[45] The SAD includes the following information for each protected connection:

- Source IP address
- Destination IP address
- SPI
- IPsec security protocol (AH or ESP)
- Mode (transport or tunnel)
- Encryption algorithm for ESP (e.g., AES-CBC)
- Integrity protection algorithm (e.g., HMAC-MD5, HMAC-SHA-1)
- Secret keys used by the selected algorithms
- Key length, if any of the selected algorithms can use multiple key sizes

---

44 By default, the shared secret created during the initial IKE SA negotiation is also used for the IPsec SAs. During quick mode, the endpoints may enable the *Perfect Forward Secrecy* (PFS) option, which causes a new shared secret to be created through a Diffie-Hellman exchange for each IPsec SA. Although PFS increases the overhead in establishing SAs, it provides greater security because each shared secret is unrelated to the others. If a shared secret were to be compromised, the attacker could not use it to gain access to data protected by any other SA.

45 Some sources use the acronym SADB for Security Association Database. This guide uses SAD, which is the acronym used in RFC 2401, *Security Architecture for the Internet Protocol* (http://www.ietf.org/rfc/rfc2401.txt).

- SA lifetime (described later in this section)
- Sequence number information
- Anti-replay information
- Types of traffic to which this SA should be applied (e.g., specific ports and/or protocols).

An SA can be uniquely identified by the combination of three parameters: the destination IP address, the SPI, and the IPsec security protocol. When an endpoint needs to know which SA applies to a particular packet, it looks it up in the SAD using these parameters. The SA describes the security measures that IPsec should use to protect communications; however, it does not fully describe what types of traffic should be protected, and under what circumstances. That information is stored in the Security Policy Database (SPD), which classifies traffic as requiring IPsec protection (*protect*), not requiring IPsec protection (*bypass*), or being prohibited (*discard*). The SPD typically contains the following information for each type of traffic that needs to be protected:

- Source and destination IP address
- IP protocol (e.g., TCP, UDP, all)
- TCP or UDP port number (optional)
- IPsec protections to be applied
- Pointer to the SA within the SAD, if an SA has already been negotiated for a particular type of traffic.

Most implementations have a GUI that enables the user to configure the SPD; the SAD entries are created as a result of IKE negotiations. In some implementations, it is not obvious how the terms used in the configuration tool match up with the SAD and SPD database entries. Both databases should be protected, and only an administrator or "super user" should be able to configure the SPD.

Both IKE and IPsec SAs typically have a limited lifetime, which cannot be increased after the SA is created. If an SA is nearing the end of its lifetime, the endpoints must create a new SA and use it instead, through a process known as *rekeying*. The *SA lifetime* specifies how often each SA should be rekeyed, either based on elapsed time or the amount of network traffic. The lifetime is most often based on an elapsed time of no more than a day. Section 4.2.5 contains additional information regarding SA lifetimes.

3.3.3 Informational Exchange

The purpose of the IKE informational exchange is to provide the endpoints a way to send each other status and error messages. The IKE SA provides protection for the status and error information, ensuring that unauthorized messages do not disrupt an IPsec negotiation or prematurely end an existing IPsec SA. For example, one endpoint can tell another endpoint that a particular SA should no longer be used. However, the messages sent through the informational exchange are UDP-based, and the recipient does not acknowledge them, so there is no guarantee that the other endpoint will receive them.

3.3.4 Group Exchange

Section 3.3.1.1 lists the pre-defined Diffie-Hellman groups. Each group number specifies a modulus size and an encryption generator type. The IKE group exchange can be used to negotiate the creation of additional Diffie-Hellman groups. Once two endpoints agree on the characteristics of a new Diffie-

Hellman group, they can specify its number in future phase one negotiations. Defining a new Diffie-Hellman group is not a trivial matter, so in practice, the group exchange is not commonly used.

3.3.5 IKE Version 2

A standard for version 2 of IKE has been in development for some time.[46] According to Appendix A of the current draft of the IKE version 2 standard, motivations for developing the version 2 standard include the following:

- Creating a single RFC that defines IKE (version 1 was defined through multiple RFCs)
- Simplifying IKE, including the elimination of extraneous features such as the aggressive and group exchanges, and authentication through public key encryption
- Establishing reliable message delivery, including acknowledged informational messages
- Providing additional protection against denial of service attacks
- Resolving issues with using IKE through NAT gateways
- Fixing bugs
- Defining how error conditions and ambigious situations should be handled.

IKE version 2 supports the Extensible Authentication Protocol (EAP), which permits IPsec to use external authentication services such as Kerberos and RADIUS. IKE version 2 also includes the Peer Authorization Database (PAD), which includes the valid identities (e.g., IP addresses) for peers and the valid authentication methods for each peer. Another significant functional difference between version 1 and version 2 is that version 2 can establish both the IKE SA and the IPsec SA in a total of 4 messages, as follows:

- In the first pair of messages, the endpoints negotiate various security parameters, as well as sending each other Diffie-Hellman values and nonces.
- In the second pair of messages, the endpoints authenticate each other and establish an IPsec SA.

Numerous IKEv2 implementations are expected to be available in 2006; it is likely that IKEv2 will be widely deployed a few years after that.

3.3.6 IKE Summary

- IPsec uses IKE to create security associations, which are sets of values that define the security of IPsec-protected connections. IKE phase 1 creates an IKE SA; IKE phase 2 creates an IPsec SA through a channel protected by the IKE SA.
- IKE phase 1 has two modes: main mode and aggressive mode. Main mode negotiates the establishment of the IKE SA through three pairs of messages, while aggressive mode uses only three messages. Although aggressive mode is faster, it is also less flexible and secure. The endpoints cannot negotiate Diffie-Hellman parameters, and identity information may not be hidden in some cases. The IKE SA created during phase 1 is bidirectional, meaning that it provides protection for both sides of the communication.

---

46 The current draft of the proposed standard for IKE version 2 is available at http://www.ietf.org/internet-drafts/draft-ietf-ipsec-ikev2-xx.txt.

- IKE phase 2 has one mode: quick mode. Quick mode uses three messages to establish the IPsec SA. Quick mode communications are encrypted by the method specified in the IKE SA created by phase 1. The IPsec SA created by phase 2 is unidirectional; therefore, a pair of SAs need to be created for each AH or ESP connection.

- The standard for version 2 of IKE is currently being finalized. It is expected to resolve several problems with the original version of IKE and to make IKE simpler and faster.

3.4 IP Payload Compression Protocol (IPComp)

In communications, it is often desirable to perform *lossless compression* on data—to repackage information in a smaller format without losing any of its meaning. For example, if host A wants to send host B a string of a thousand X's, it would be more efficient to send host B a single X and tell it to use a thousand of them. Similarly, using a compression protocol for IPsec communications should improve the efficiency of IPsec in terms of network bandwidth because fewer bytes of data will need to be transmitted. However, there is a problem with this. Ideally, the process of encryption makes data appear random to an observer; for example, the letters, digits and punctuation of an email message may be converted into many different printable and non-printable characters. Random data is very difficult to compress, because compression works by communicating the same information in a smaller format. Therefore, it is much more effective to first compress data and then encrypt it.

The IP Payload Compression Protocol (IPComp)[47] is often used with IPsec.[48] By applying IPComp to a payload first, then encrypting the packet through ESP, effective compression can be achieved. However, this is somewhat dependent on the data in each packet. For example, compression provides little savings on very small payloads. Also, some data may already be compressed by an application or other means. In these cases, it is a waste of resources to compress the payload, as the overhead of compressing and decompressing the data outweighs the benefit of a trivial reduction in payload size (or no reduction at all). Accordingly, IPComp only uses compression if it actually makes the packet smaller. If it attempts to compress a packet and discovers that no benefit is gained, it will send the original, non-compressed packet so that the receiver does not waste resources performing decompression.

Each packet that has had compression applied will contain an IPComp header. Each header has three fields:

- **Next Header.** This field contains the IP protocol number for the packet payload, such as 6 for TCP or 17 for UDP.

- **Reserved.** This field is reserved for future use, so it should be set to 0.

- **Compression Parameter Index (CPI).** This is similar to the SPI. The CPI and the destination IP address form a *compression security association.*

IPComp can be configured to provide compression for IPsec traffic going in one direction only (e.g., compress packets from endpoint A to endpoint B, but not from endpoint B to endpoint A) or in both directions. Also, IPComp allows administrators to choose from multiple compression algorithms,

---

[47] IPComp uses IP protocol number 108. Another acronym used for the IP Payload Compression Protocol is PCP. This guide uses IPComp, which is the acronym used in RFC 3173, *IP Payload Compression Protocol* (http://www.ietf.org/rfc/rfc3173.txt).

[48] The use of IPComp can be negotiated through IKE, along with the IPsec protocols.

including DEFLATE and LZS.[49] IPComp provides a simple yet flexible solution for compressing IPsec payloads.

3.5 Putting It All Together

Sections 3.1 through 3.4 present the primary components of IPsec—AH, ESP, and IKE—and IPComp. This section puts those components together to illustrate how IPsec sessions are set up and executed. Each example includes the use of IKE to establish security associations. The first scenario involves using ESP in a gateway-to-gateway architecture, while the second scenario looks at providing both IPComp and ESP services in a host-to-gateway architecture. The final scenario describes using ESP and AH in a host-to-host architecture.

3.5.1 ESP in a Gateway-to-Gateway Architecture

In this scenario, the goal is to establish an IPsec connection that provides encryption and integrity protection services between endpoints A and B. The IPsec architecture is gateway-to-gateway; endpoint A uses gateway A on network A, and endpoint B uses gateway B on network B. The first step in establishing the connection is to create an IKE SA (if one does not already exist), as follows:

1. Endpoint A creates and sends a regular (non-IPsec) packet that has a destination address of endpoint B.

2. Network A routes the packet to gateway A.

3. Gateway A receives the packet and performs NAT, altering the packet's source IP address.

4. Gateway A matches the packet's characteristics against those in its Security Policy Database. It determines that the packet should be protected by encryption and integrity protection through ESP, and also determines the address of the destination gateway. Because the SPD entry does not have a pointer to an IKE SA, it knows that no IKE SA currently exists to protect this particular traffic.

5. Gateway A initiates an IKE SA negotiation with Gateway B using either main mode or aggressive mode. At the end of the negotiation, the IKE SA is created.

The next step in establishing the ESP connection is to create IPsec SAs, as follows:

6. Gateway A uses the parameters set in the IKE SA to initiate an IPsec SA negotiation with gateway B. The IKE SA provides protection for the negotiation, which is performed using quick mode. The parameters specify that ESP tunnel mode will be used and that it will provide encryption and integrity protection. At the end of the negotiation, a pair of unidirectional IPsec SAs is created for the ESP tunnel. Each SA provides protection only for traffic going in one direction.

7. Once the two IPsec SAs have been created, gateway A can finish processing the packet sent by endpoint A in step 1. The packet will first be encrypted, then processed for integrity protection. The following steps outline how the data actually reaches its destination:

---

[49] Section 4.4.5 of RFC 2407, *The Internet IP Security Domain of Interpretation for ISAKMP*, contains a list of supported compression algorithms. The RFC is available at http://www.ietf.org/rfc/rfc2407.txt. More information on specific algorithms is available in RFC 2394 (*IP Payload Compression Using DEFLATE*, at http://www.ietf.org/rfc/rfc2394.txt) and RFC 2395 (*IP Payload Compression Using LZS*, at http://www.ietf.org/rfc/rfc2395.txt).

a. Gateway A modifies the packet so it is protected in accordance with the SA parameters. This includes adding a new IP packet header that uses gateway A's IP address as the source IP address, and gateway B's IP address as the destination address, encrypting the data, then adding the authentication information. Gateway A then sends the packet to Gateway B.

b. Gateway B receives the packet and uses the value in the unencrypted SPI field from the ESP header to determine which SA should be applied to the packet. After looking up the SA parameters (including the secret keys needed for integrity protection and decryption), gateway B processes and validates the packet. This includes removing the additional IP packet header, checking the integrity of the encrypted data, optionally performing a replay check, and decrypting the original payload. Gateway B checks the SPD to ensure that the required protections were applied to the packet, then sends the packet to its actual destination, endpoint B.

If endpoint B wishes to reply to the packet, the last step of this process is repeated, except the parties are switched. Endpoint B would send a packet to endpoint A; routing would direct it to gateway B. Gateway B would modify the packet appropriately and send it to gateway A. Gateway A would process and validate the packet, apply NAT to restore the original IP address, then send the packet to endpoint A.

Assuming that the IPsec connection between the gateways is sustained, eventually the IKE or IPsec SAs will approach one of the SA lifetime thresholds (maximum time, maximum bytes transmitted). The first gateway that determines the SA lifetime is approaching initiates the rekeying process. This causes some of the steps listed previously to be performed again, depending on which type of SAs (IKE or IPsec) needs to be rekeyed. Once the new SAs have been created, the gateways send all new traffic over the new SAs, and eventually the old SAs are deleted. (The precise details of the rekeying process can vary significantly among IPsec implementations.)

3.5.2 ESP and IPComp in a Host-to-Gateway Architecture

In this scenario, the goal is to establish an IPsec connection that provides encryption, integrity protection, and compression services between endpoints A and B. The IPsec architecture is host-to-gateway; endpoint A is located on network A, and endpoint B uses gateway B on network B. The first step in establishing the connection is to create an IKE SA, as follows:

1. Endpoint A creates a regular (non-IPsec) packet that has a destination address of endpoint B. When endpoint A attempts to send this packet, its IPsec client software matches its characteristics against those in its Security Policy Database and determines that ESP and IPComp should be applied to the packet. It also determines the IP address of the destination gateway, Gateway B.

2. Endpoint A initiates an IKE SA negotiation with Gateway B using either main mode or aggressive mode. At the end of the negotiation, the IKE SA is created.

The next step in establishing the ESP and IPComp connection is to create IPsec SAs, as follows:

3. Endpoint A uses the parameters set in the IKE SA to initiate an IPsec SA negotiation with gateway B. The IKE SA provides protection for the negotiation, which is performed using quick mode. The parameters specify that ESP tunnel mode will be used and that it will provide both encryption and integrity protection, and that IPComp will also be applied. At the end of the negotiation, a pair of unidirectional IPsec SAs is created for the tunnel, as well as a pair of IPComp SAs.

Once the two IPsec SAs have been created, endpoint A can finish processing the initial packet. The following steps outline how the data actually reaches its destination:

4. Endpoint A modifies the packet so it is protected in accordance with the SA parameters. IPComp is applied first, then ESP. This includes adding a new IP packet header that uses gateway B's IP address as the destination address. Endpoint A then sends the packet to Gateway B.

5. Gateway B receives the packet and uses the value in the unencrypted SPI field from the ESP header to determine which SA should be applied to the packet. After looking up the SA parameters, gateway B processes and validates the packet. This includes removing the additional IP packet header, decompressing the data (if necessary), performing the integrity verification, optionally performing a replay check, and decrypting the original payload. Gateway B checks the SPD to ensure that the policy was followed properly, then sends the packet to its actual destination, endpoint B.

If endpoint B wishes to reply to the packet, the last two steps of this process are repeated, except the parties are switched. Endpoint B would send a packet to endpoint A; routing would direct it to gateway B. Gateway B would modify the packet appropriately and send it to endpoint A.

3.5.3 ESP and AH in a Host-to-Host Architecture

In this scenario, the goal is to establish a transport mode IPsec connection that provides encryption and authentication between endpoints A and B. Because of security concerns, AH authentication has been selected instead of ESP authentication because AH can check the integrity of the IP header. The IPsec architecture is host-to-host, with both endpoints on the same network. The first step in establishing the connection is to create an IKE SA, as follows:

1. Endpoint A creates a regular (non-IPsec) packet that has a destination address of endpoint B. When endpoint A attempts to send this packet, its IPsec client software matches its characteristics against those in its Security Policy Database and determines that ESP and AH should be applied to the packet. It also determines that the packet should be sent to endpoint B (e.g., no need to change the address to point to an IPsec gateway).

2. Endpoint A initiates an IKE SA negotiation with endpoint B using either main mode or aggressive mode. At the end of the negotiation, the IKE SA is created.

The next step in establishing the ESP and AH connection is to create IPsec SAs, as follows:

3. Endpoint A uses the parameters set in the IKE SA to initiate an IPsec SA negotiation with endpoint B for the AH service. The IKE SA provides protection for the negotiation, which is performed using quick mode. The parameters specify that AH transport mode will be used. At the end of the negotiation, a pair of unidirectional SAs is created for the tunnel.

4. Step 3 is repeated to negotiate the SAs for the ESP service.[50]

Once the four IPsec SAs have been created, endpoint A can finish processing the initial packet. The following steps outline how the data actually reaches its destination:

---

50 Some IPsec implementations follow this model—establishing two separate, unconnected SAs—while other IPsec implementations link the two SAs together to form an *SA bundle*. A bundle provides a convenient way for IPsec to apply multiple types of protection to traffic. However, the use of bundles sometimes causes interoperability problems because it has not been implemented consistently in IPsec software.

5. Endpoint A modifies the packet so it is protected in accordance with the SA parameters. ESP is applied first, then AH. (This allows AH to provide integrity for the ESP portions of the packet.) Endpoint A then sends the packet to endpoint B.

6. Endpoint B receives the packet and uses the SPI value from the AH header to determine which SA should be applied to the packet. After looking up the SA parameters, endpoint B processes and validates the packet, in terms of AH. Next, Endpoint B uses the value in the unencrypted SPI field from the ESP header to determine which SA should be applied to the packet next. After looking up the SA parameters, endpoint B processes and validates the packet, in terms of ESP. The IPsec client on endpoint B then releases the packet so the host can process it.

If endpoint B wishes to reply to the packet, the last two steps of this process are repeated, except the parties are switched. Endpoint B would create a packet and send it directly to endpoint A.

3.6 Summary

This section has described the AH, ESP, IKE, and IPComp protocols, and demonstrated how they work together to create IPsec-protected connections and to provide encryption, integrity protection, and compression services for those connections. The following summarizes the key points from the section:

- AH provides integrity protection for all packet headers and data, with the exception of a few IP header fields that routinely change unpredictably in transit. Because AH includes source and destination IP addresses in its calculations, AH is incompatible with NAT. The usage of AH has decreased because the second version of ESP, which is the current version, can now provide integrity protection services as well. However, ESP cannot provide the integrity check for the outermost IP header that AH can.

- In tunnel mode, ESP can provide encryption and integrity protection for an encapsulated IP packet and the ESP trailer, as well as integrity protection for the ESP header. ESP tunnel mode is the most commonly used IPsec mode. Because it can encrypt the original IP header, it can conceal the true source and destination of the packet. Also, ESP can add padding to packets, further complicating attempts to perform traffic analysis. Another strength of ESP tunnel mode is that it can be compatible with NAT.

- In transport mode, ESP can provide encryption and integrity protection for the payload of an IP packet, and the ESP header and trailer. Transport mode is not compatible with NAT.

- IPsec uses IKE to create security associations, which are sets of values that define the security of IPsec-protected connections. IKE phase 1 creates an IKE SA; IKE phase 2 creates an IPsec SA through a channel protected by the IKE SA. IKE phase 1 has two modes: main mode and aggressive mode. Main mode negotiates the establishment of the bidirectional IKE SA through three pairs of messages, while aggressive mode uses only three messages. Although aggressive mode is faster, it is also less flexible and secure. IKE phase 2 has one mode: quick mode. Quick mode uses three messages to establish a pair of unidirectional IPsec SAs. Quick mode communications are encrypted by the method specified in the IKE SA created by phase 1.

- IPComp can provide lossless compression for IPsec payloads. Because applying compression algorithms to certain types of payloads may actually make them larger, IPComp only compresses the payload if it will actually make the packet smaller.

4. IPsec Planning and Implementation

This section focuses on the planning and implementation of IPsec in the enterprise. As with any new technology deployment, IPsec planning and implementation should be addressed in a phased approach. A successful deployment of IPsec can be achieved by following a clear, step-by-step planning and implementation process. The use of a phased approach for deployment can minimize unforeseen issues and identify potential pitfalls early in the process. This model also allows for the incorporation of advances in new technology, as well as adapting IPsec to the ever-changing enterprise. This section explores in depth each of the IPsec planning and implementation phases, as follows:

1. **Identify Needs.** The first phase of the process involves identifying the need to protect network communications, determining which computers, networks, and data are part of the communications, and identifying related requirements (e.g., minimum performance). This phase also involves determining how that need can best be met (e.g., IPsec, SSL, SSH) and deciding where and how the security should be implemented.

2. **Design the Solution.** The second phase involves all facets of designing the IPsec solution. For simplicity, the design elements are grouped into four categories: architectural considerations, authentication methods, cryptography policy, and packet filters.

3. **Implement and Test a Prototype.** The next phase involves implementing and testing a prototype of the designed solution in a lab or test environment. The primary goals of the testing are to evaluate the functionality, performance, scalability, and security of the solution, and to identify any issues with the components, such as interoperability issues.

4. **Deploy the Solution.** Once the testing is completed and all issues are resolved, the next phase includes the gradual deployment of IPsec throughout the enterprise.

5. **Manage the Solution.** After the IPsec solution has been deployed, it is managed throughout its lifecycle. Management includes maintenance of the IPsec components and support for operational issues. The lifecycle process is repeated when enhancements or significant changes need to be incorporated into the solution.

Organizations should also implement other measures that support and complement IPsec implementations. These measures help to ensure that IPsec is implemented in an environment with the technical, management, and operational controls necessary to provide adequate security for the IPsec implementation. Examples of supporting measures are as follows:

- Establish and maintain control over all entry and exit points for the protected network, which helps to ensure its integrity.
- Ensure that all IPsec endpoints (gateways and hosts) are secured and maintained properly, which should reduce the risk of IPsec compromise or misuse.
- Revise organizational policies as needed to incorporate appropriate usage of the IPsec solution. Policies should provide the foundation for the planning and implementation of IPsec. Appendix A contains extensive discussion of IPsec-related policy considerations.

4.1 Identify Needs

The purpose of this phase is to identify the need to protect communications and determine how that need can best be met. The first step is to determine which communications need to be protected (e.g., all communications between two networks, certain applications involving a particular server). The next step is to determine what protection measures (e.g., providing confidentiality, assuring integrity, authenticating the source) are needed for each type of communication. It is also important to identify other general and application-specific requirements, such as performance, and to think about future needs. For example, if it is likely that other types of communications will need protection in a year, those needs should also be considered.

After identifying all the relevant needs, the organization should consider the possible technical solutions and select the one that best meets the identified needs. Although IPsec is typically a reasonable choice, other protocols such as SSL or SSH may be equally good or better in some cases. See Section 5 for descriptions of such protocols and guidance on when a particular protocol may be a viable alternative to IPsec. In some cases, IPsec is the only option—for example, if a gateway-to-gateway VPN is being established with a business partner that has already purchased and deployed an IPsec gateway for the connection. Another possibility is that the solution may need to support a protocol that is only provided by IPsec; for example, Section 3.1 mentions that some protocols require the use of AH. Assuming that IPsec is chosen as the solution's protocol, the Identify Needs phase should result in the following:

- Identification of all communications that need to be protected (e.g., servers, client hosts, networks, applications, data), and the protection that each type of communication needs (preferably encryption, integrity protection, and peer authentication)
- Selection of an IPsec architecture model (e.g., gateway-to-gateway, host-to-gateway, host-to-host)
- Specification of performance requirements (normal and peak loads).

4.2 Design the Solution

Once the needs have been identified and it has been determined that IPsec is the best solution, the next phase is to design a solution that meets the needs. This involves four major components, which are described in more detail in Sections 4.2.1 through 4.2.4:

- **Architecture.** Designing the architecture of the IPsec implementation includes host placement (for host-to-host architectures)[51] and gateway placement (for host-to-gateway and gateway-to-gateway architectures), IPsec client software selection (for host-to-host and host-to-gateway architectures), and host address space management considerations (for host-to-host and host-to-gateway architectures).
- **Authentication.** The IPsec implementation must have an authentication method selected, such as pre-shared key or digital signature.
- **Cryptography.** The algorithms for encryption and integrity protection must be selected, as well as the key strength for algorithms that support multiple key lengths.
- **Packet Filter.** The packet filter determines which types of traffic should be permitted and denied, and what protection and compression measures (if any) should be applied to each type of permitted traffic (e.g., ESP tunnel using AES for encryption and HMAC-SHA-1 for integrity protection; LZS for compression).

[51] In most cases, the hosts are already placed on the network; the architectural considerations are focused on identifying intermediate devices between the hosts, such as firewalls performing NAT.

The decisions made regarding authentication, cryptography, and packet filters are all documented in the IPsec policy. In its simplest form, an IPsec policy is a set of rules that govern the use of the IPsec protocol. It specifies the data to secure and the security method to use to secure that data. An IPsec policy determines the type of traffic that is allowed through IPsec endpoints, and generally consists of a packet filter and a set of security parameters for traffic that matches the packet filter. Those parameters include the authentication and encryption scheme and tunnel settings. When communications occur, each packet filter can result in the establishment of one or more SAs that enable protected communications satisfying the security policy for that packet filter.

Other decisions should also be made during the design phase, such as setting IKE and IPsec SA lifetimes, choosing main or aggressive mode for the IKE phase one exchange, and identifying which Diffie-Hellman group number is best. Besides meeting the organization's authentication and cryptography requirements, design decisions should incorporate the organization's logging and data management strategies, incident response and recovery plans, resource replication and failover needs, and current and future network characteristics, such as the use of wireless, NAT, and IPv6. Section 4.2.5 covers these considerations and design decisions in more detail.

4.2.1 Architecture

The architecture of the IPsec implementation refers to the selection of devices and software to provide IPsec services and the placement of IPsec endpoints within the existing network infrastructure. These two considerations are often closely tied together; for example, a decision could be made to use the existing Internet firewall as the IPsec gateway. This section will explore three particular aspects of IPsec architecture: gateway placement, IPsec client software for hosts, and host address space management.

4.2.1.1 Gateway Placement

Due to the layered defense strategy used to protect enterprise networks, IPsec gateway placement is often a challenging task. As described later in this section, the gateway's placement has security, functionality, and performance implications. Also, the gateway's placement may have an effect on other network devices, such as firewalls, routers, and switches. Incorporating an IPsec gateway into a network architecture requires strong overall knowledge of the network and security policy. The following are major factors to consider for IPsec gateway placement:

- **Device Performance.** IPsec can be computationally intensive, primarily because of encryption and decryption. Providing IPsec services from another device (e.g., firewall, router) may put too high of a load on the device during peak usage, causing service disruptions. A possible alternative is to offload the cryptography operations to a specialized hardware device, such as a card with built-in cryptography functions. Organizations should also review their network architecture to determine if bottlenecks are likely to occur due to network devices (e.g., routers, firewalls) that cannot sustain the processing of peak volumes of network traffic that includes IPsec-encapsulated packets.[52]

- **Traffic Examination.** If IPsec-encrypted traffic passes through a firewall, it cannot tell what protocols the packets' payloads contain, so it cannot filter the traffic based on those protocols. Intrusion detection systems encounter the same issue; they cannot examine encrypted traffic for attacks. It is generally recommended to design the IPsec architecture so that a firewall and intrusion detection software can examine the unencrypted traffic. Organizations most commonly

[52] The network architecture review is also beneficial in identifying intermediate network devices that may need to be reconfigured to permit IPsec traffic to pass through.

address this by using their Internet firewalls as VPN gateways or placing VPN gateway devices just outside their Internet firewalls.

- **Traffic Not Protected by IPsec.** Organizations should consider carefully the threats against network traffic after it has been processed by the receiving IPsec gateway and sent without IPsec protection across additional network segments. For example, an organization that wants to place its VPN gateway outside its Internet firewalls should ensure that the traffic passing between the IPsec gateway and the Internet firewalls has sufficient protection against breaches of confidentiality and integrity.

- **Gateway Outages.** The architecture should take into consideration the effects of IPsec gateway outages, including planned maintenance outages and unplanned outages caused by failures or attacks. For example, if the IPsec gateway is placed inline near the Internet connection point, meaning that all network traffic passes through it, a gateway failure could cause a loss of all Internet connectivity for the organization. Also, larger IPsec implementations may use a gateway management server; a server failure could severely impact management of all gateways. Generally, if the network is designed to be redundant, the IPsec gateways and management servers should also be designed to be redundant.

- **NAT.** NAT provides a mechanism to use private addresses on the internal network while using public addresses to connect to external networks. NAT can map each private address to a different public address, while the Network Address Port Translation (NAPT) variant of NAT can map many private addresses to a single public address, differentiating the original addresses by assigning different public address ports.[53] NAT is often used by enterprises, small offices, and residential users that do not want to pay for more IP addresses than necessary or wish to take advantage of the security benefits and flexibility of having private addresses assigned to internal hosts. Unfortunately, as described in Section 3, there are known incompatibilities between IPsec and NAT because NAT modifies the IP addresses in the packet, which directly violates the packet integrity assurance provided by IPsec. However, there are a few solutions to this issue, as follows:

  – Perform NAT before applying IPsec. This can be accomplished by arranging the devices in a particular order, or by using an IPsec gateway that also performs NAT. For example, the gateway can perform NAT first and then IPsec for outbound packets.

  – Use UDP encapsulation of ESP packets. UDP encapsulation can be used with tunnel mode ESP or Layer 2 Tunneling Protocol (L2TP) (as described in Section 4.2.1.3) over transport mode ESP. UDP encapsulation appends a UDP header to each packet, which provides an IP address and UDP port that can be used by NAT (including NAPT). This removes conflicts between IPsec and NAT in most environments.[54] An IKE enhancement known as IPsec NAT Traversal (NAT-T) allows IKE to negotiate the use of UDP encapsulation. During the IKE phase one exchange, both endpoints declare their support of NAT-T through a vendor ID payload (containing the hash of a well-known vendor ID value and static phrase), then perform NAT discovery to determine if NAT services are running between the two IPsec endpoints. NAT discovery involves each endpoint sending a hash of its original source address and port to the other endpoint, which compares the original values to the actual

[53] Additional information on NAT and NAPT is available from RFC 2663, *IP Network Address Translator (NAT) Terminology and Considerations*, available at http://www.ietf.org/rfc/rfc2663.txt.

[54] In some cases, either the network architecture or the type of traffic may require additional measures to allow IPsec traffic to negotiate NAT successfully. For example, protocols such as Session Initiation Protocol (SIP) for Voice over IP (VoIP) and File Transfer Protocol (FTP) have IP addresses embedded in the application data. Handling such traffic correctly in NAT environments may require the use of application layer gateways (ALG).

values to determine if NAT was applied. IKE then moves its communications from UDP port 500 to port 4500, to avoid inadvertent interference from NAT devices that perform proprietary alterations of IPsec-related activity. NAT-T can also cause the host to send keepalive packets to the other endpoint, which should keep the NAPT port-to-address mapping from being lost. Although UDP encapsulation and NAT-T can be helpful in overcoming NAT-related issues, not all IPsec software and hardware devices support them at this time.[55]

– At small or home offices, configure cable and Digital Subscriber Line (DSL) routers performing NAT to permit IPsec NAT pass-through for the IPsec client systems.

4.2.1.2 IPsec Client Software for Hosts

In IPsec host-to-host and host-to-gateway architectures, each host must have an IPsec-compliant client installed and configured. Many operating systems have built-in IPsec clients; several IPsec vendors and other organizations (e.g., open source developers) also provide their own IPsec clients for various operating systems.[56] Built-in clients simply need to be configured, while third-party clients must be distributed and installed, then configured.[57] However, third-party clients may support features that the built-in clients do not, which may provide sufficient justification for using a third-party client instead of a built-in client. Features that may be of interest when evaluating IPsec client software include support for the following:

- Particular encryption, integrity protection, and compression algorithms
- Particular authentication methods
- Multiple simultaneous tunnels[58]
- Automatic rekeying[59]
- AH
- IKE phase one aggressive mode
- L2TP (described in Section 4.2.1.3)
- Certificates/certificate revocation lists (CRL).

Another important IPsec client feature is the ability to prevent split tunneling. Split tunneling occurs when an IPsec client on an external network is not configured to send all its traffic to the organization's IPsec gateway. Requests with a destination on the organization's network are sent to the IPsec gateway,

---

[55] For more information, see RFC 3947, *Negotiation of NAT-Traversal in the IKE*, available at http://www.ietf.org/rfc/rfc3947.txt, and RFC 3948, *UDP Encapsulation of IPsec Packets*, available at http://www.ietf.org/rfc/rfc3948.txt. The standards do not specify any support for UDP encapsulation of AH packets.

[56] Built-in IPsec clients are typically part of the IP stack. Third-party clients are typically *shims*, which means that they are implemented between the IP stack and the local network drivers. This technique is also known as a "bump in the stack" (BITS). Historically, shim clients tended to be more problematic than built-in clients because of incompatibilities between the shim and the operating system, but generally this is no longer true.

[57] Organizations implementing third-party clients should pay particular attention to the clients' hardware and software requirements. Some systems may not be capable of running certain clients, while other systems may need to be upgraded.

[58] In some cases, it may be desirable to permit a host to establish multiple tunnels simultaneously. For example, the host may perform two types of communications that each need different protective measures from IPsec.

[59] Some clients do not support automatic rekeying; when an SA expires, the IPsec connection is lost and the user needs to initiate a new connection. This is unlikely to be an issue if most IPsec sessions are short in duration (e.g., a few hours long). Section 3.3.2 contains additional information on rekeying.

and all other requests are sent directly to their destination without going through the IPsec tunnel. The client host is effectively communicating directly and simultaneously with the organization's internal network and another network (typically the Internet). If the client host were compromised, a remote attacker could connect to the host surreptitiously and use its IPsec tunnel to gain unauthorized access to the organization's network. This would not be possible if the IPsec client software had been configured to prohibit split tunneling. However, any compromise of an IPsec client host is problematic, because an attacker could install utilities on the host that capture data, passwords, and other valuable information.

Prohibiting split tunneling can limit the potential impact of a compromise by preventing the attacker from taking advantage of the IPsec connection to enter the organization's network; the attacker could only connect to the compromised system when it is not using IPsec. However, many hosts have multiple methods of connectivity, such as dial-up, wired LAN, and wireless LAN; if an attacker can connect to a network interface other than the one used for IPsec, it may be possible to use the IPsec tunnel even if split tunneling is prohibited. This can allow access to a more trusted network—the network protected by IPsec—from a less trusted network, such as an improperly secured wireless LAN. Accordingly, hosts should be configured so that only the network interface used for IPsec is enabled when IPsec is in use. Some VPN clients can be configured to disable other network interfaces automatically. An alternative is to configure a personal firewall on the host so that it blocks unnecessary and unauthorized network traffic on all interfaces. As described in Section 4.2.5, this is also helpful in preventing IPsec clients' hosts from being compromised.

There are other factors that may differentiate IPsec clients. For example, one client may provide substantially better performance than another client or consume less of the host's resources. Another consideration is the security of the client software itself, such as how frequently vulnerabilities are identified, and how quickly patches are available. Client interoperability with other IPsec implementations is also a key concern; many client implementations only interoperate with their own vendor's gateway implementation or with a limited number of other vendors' gateway implementations. It is critical to ensure that the selected client will interoperate with each gateway implementation that it might encounter. Section 4.3.1 discusses this topic in more detail.

Organizations should also carefully consider how clients can be provisioned with IPsec client software and configuration settings, including policies. Many clients offer different features that can make client deployment, configuration, and management easier. For example, an administrator might be able to set policy for clients remotely, instead of manually visiting each host. Some clients offer administrators the ability to lock out or disable certain configuration options or functionality so that users cannot inadvertently or intentionally circumvent the intended security. If administrators cannot distribute pre-configured IPsec clients or remotely control IPsec configuration settings, then the administrators might need to manually configure each IPsec client or rely on users to follow instructions and configure the clients themselves. The latter approach is often challenging because of the complexity for the typical users of configuring an IPsec client.

4.2.1.3 Host Address Space Management

In IPsec architectures where the hosts are outside the organization (e.g., telecommuters, road warriors), by default the hosts will have IP addresses that are outside the organization's address ranges. If the organization has implemented internal security measures based on IP addresses, then IPsec hosts may not be able to access these internal computing resources. Assuming that the organization wants the IPsec hosts to access such resources, it can either alter its security controls so that they are not based on IP addresses, or have an additional IP address from the organization's address space assigned as a virtual IP address to each external IPsec host. In the latter case, the client then establishes an IPsec connection that uses its real IP address in the external packet headers (so the IPsec-encapsulated packets can be routed across public networks) and its virtual IP address in the internal packet headers (so the packets can be routed across the organization's internal networks and treated as internally generated).

Virtual addresses are typically assigned by a Dynamic Host Configuration Protocol (DHCP) server or the IPsec gateway, using a range of addresses designated for IPsec clients. They may also be assigned by DHCP and transmitted to the host by the IPsec gateway. Assignment by the IPsec gateway provides more control over the remote access clients and allows administrators to quickly determine whether the source of a connection is an internal host or an external IPsec client. It is important to ensure that any addresses that the IPsec gateway manages are excluded from the ranges that other internal DHCP servers can assign to avoid address conflicts.

Some vendors provide internal address assignment and authentication using proprietary functionality. This may present compatibility issues depending on the products being used. In other cases, IPsec should be used with Layer Two Tunneling Protocol (L2TP) to provide secure remote access to enterprises.[60] L2TP, which is documented in RFC 2661,[61] is an extension of the Point-to-Point Tunneling Protocol (PPTP) that can be used by an ISP to provide VPN connections. L2TP is easily integrated with DHCP to provide automatic IP address assignment to IPsec client machines.

The following illustrates the typical process of establishing an L2TP/IPsec session, assuming that the host is using IPsec client software that supports L2TP/IPsec sessions:

1. The host connects to its ISP and is assigned a regular IP address.
2. The host then initiates an IPsec connection with the organization's IPsec gateway. This leads to the creation of IPsec SAs to provide ESP transport mode connections between the host and gateway.
3. Next, the host establishes an L2TP tunnel, protected by IPsec, between itself and the organization's IPsec gateway. This results in the gateway assigning a virtual IP address to the host.

The host can now use its virtual IP address to communicate with the IPsec gateway. The packets sent between the host and gateway use several levels of encapsulation, as follows:

1. **Point-to-Point Protocol (PPP) Encapsulation.** The initial IP payload is encapsulated with PPP, as is typical with any communications between the host and the ISP.
2. **L2TP Encapsulation.** The packet is next encapsulated with an L2TP header.
3. **UDP Encapsulation.** The L2TP-encapsulated packet is next encapsulated with a UDP header containing the appropriate source and destination ports. (L2TP uses UDP port 1701.)
4. **IPsec Encapsulation.** Based on the IPsec policy, the UDP message is encrypted and encapsulated with an ESP header and trailer.
5. **IP Encapsulation.** The IPsec packet is encapsulated with a final IP header containing the source and destination IP addresses of the IPsec client and gateway.

---

60 For more information on using IPsec and L2TP together (sometimes known as L2TP/IPsec), see RFC 2888: *Secure Remote Access With L2TP* (http://www.ietf.org/rfc/rfc2888.txt) and RFC 3193: *Securing L2TP Using IPsec* (http://www.ietf.org/rfc/rfc3193.txt).

61 RFC 2661, *Layer Two Tunneling Protocol*, is available at http://www.ietf.org/rfc/rfc2661.txt.

L2TP/IPsec is most commonly used when an organization contracts VPN services from an ISP. L2TP provides a solution for assigning IP addresses to hosts, while IPsec provides strong protection for the network traffic. In most other environments, IPsec and L2TP/IPsec can both provide sufficient protection for traffic, so IPsec alone is used because of its relative simplicity and lower overhead.

4.2.2 Authentication

As described in Section 3.3.1.1, the endpoints of an IPsec connection use the same authentication method to validate each other. IPsec implementations typically support two authentication methods: pre-shared keys and digital signatures. This section discusses the primary advantages and disadvantages of these methods.[62]

To use pre-shared keys, the IPsec administrator creates a key or password string, which is then configured in each IPsec device.[63] Pre-shared keys are the simplest authentication method to implement, but key management is challenging. Administrators need to find IPsec products that provide key management capabilities for the pre-shared keys (in addition to IKE, which negotiates and manages the IPsec secret keys) or implement their own key management mechanisms, such as generating, storing, deploying, auditing, and destroying keys; proper key management can be quite resource-intensive. Although it is easiest to create a single key that is shared by all endpoints, this causes problems when a host should no longer have access—the key then needs to be changed on all hosts immediately. Keys should also be updated periodically to reduce the potential impact of a compromised key. Another issue is that the key must be kept secret and transferred over secure channels. Individuals with access to an endpoint may be able to gain access to the pre-shared key. Depending on the key type, this could grant access from one, some, or all IP addresses. (A group shared key can only be used from addresses in a certain range, while a wildcard shared key can be used from any IP address.) Also, using the same key for a group of endpoints reduces accountability and provides no replay protection.

Because of scalability and security concerns, pre-shared key authentication is generally an acceptable solution only for small-scale implementations with known IP addresses or small IP address ranges. The use of a single pre-shared key for a group of hosts is strongly discouraged for all but the most highly-controlled environments, such as a group of secure routers. Pre-shared keys are also generally not recommended for use with hosts that have dynamic IP addresses, such as telecommuters and road warriors, because the keys cannot be restricted to a particular IP address or small range of IP addresses. Pre-shared keys are also frequently used during initial IPsec testing and implementation because of their simplicity. After the IPsec implementation is operating properly, the authentication method can then be changed.

In the digital signature method, a certificate identifies each device, and each device is configured to use certificates. (User-specific certificates may be used instead of device-specific certificates.) Two IPsec endpoints will trust each other if a Certification Authority (CA) that they both trust has signed their certificates.[64] The certificates must be securely stored in the local certificate store on the IPsec hosts and gateways or on a secure token. Using a certificate-based method allows much of the key administration to be offloaded to a central certificate server, but still requires IPsec administrators to perform some key management activities, such as provisioning hosts with credentials, either through IPsec vendor-provided features or IPsec administrator-created capabilities. Many organizations are currently implementing public key infrastructures (PKI) for managing certificates for IPsec VPNs and other applications such as

[62] As described in Section 3.3.5, IKE version 2 supports the use of EAP as an authentication method. IKEv2 also allows the peers to use different authentication methods.

[63] Because pre-shared keys are often long strings of random characters, manually typing them in to the endpoints can cause problems from typos.

[64] This describes the most common CA model; other models, such as the Federal Bridge CA, function somewhat differently.

secure e-mail and Web access.[65] Section 7.3 describes an IETF working group that is developing standards for PKI and IPsec interoperability.[66]

Although the digital signature method scales well to large implementations and generally provides a more secure solution than pre-shared keys, it does have some disadvantages. For example, the IPsec implementation should perform validity and revocation checking whenever a digital certificate is used; unfortunately, the IKE negotiation may time out while the checks are occurring. Also, current standards do not specify a method for checking for revoked certificates; the most commonly used options are the Online Certificate Status Protocol (OCSP),[67] which can check the status of certificates on an on-demand basis, and Certificate Revocation Lists (CRL),[68] which maintain certificate status information on the client and typically only perform status updates occasionally.

Another potential problem with the digital signature method involves packet fragmentation. Packets in an IKE negotiation are typically relatively small and do not need to be fragmented. By adding certificates to the negotiation, packets may become so large that they need to be fragmented, which is not handled well by some IPsec implementations in all cases. Organizations also need to determine an effective method for provisioning IPsec hosts with digital certificates. The current standards do not specify a provisioning method, so IPsec implementations may support various methods, such as using Hypertext Transfer Protocol (HTTP) or Lightweight Directory Access Protocol (LDAP).

Some IPsec implementations also support the use of legacy asymmetric authentication servers such as Terminal Access Controller Access Control System (TACACS) and RADIUS. Many organizations have already made considerable investments into these authentication mechanisms (sometimes including the deployment of authentication token devices across the enterprise), and they can provide authentication for hosts and gateways. However, support for such authentication mechanisms is not mandated by current IPsec standards, so organizations may experience difficulties in finding IPsec clients and servers that are fully interoperable with each other in using the authentication mechanism. Also, asymmetric authentication has a significant security weakness—the client authenticates the gateway, then uses that channel to authenticate the client. Asymmetric authentication is susceptible to known attacks.

The Pre-IKE Credential (PIC) Provisioning Protocol was intended to provide a way to convert legacy authentication credentials to a format that is supported by the IKE standard, such as a pre-shared key or a digital certificate. Users would authenticate to a legacy authentication server, which would then use the Extensible Authentication Protocol (EAP)[69] to transport the credentials to a regular (non-legacy) authentication server. This server would process the credentials and provide an IKE-accepted credential for IPsec authentication. The PIC protocol has not been commonly used because it was viewed as too cumbersome and required additional investments in authentication mechanisms. However, as mentioned in Section 3.3.5, EAP support is included as part of the proposed IKE version 2 standard. The standard supports older and newer EAP methods, providing one-way or mutual authentication for IPsec endpoints. If a one-way method is used to authenticate the initiator (typically a road warrior) to the responder

---

65 PKI implementations require a considerable investment in time and resources. It is outside the scope of this document to discuss PKI in detail. See NIST Special Publication 800-32, *Introduction to Public Key Technology and the Federal PKI Infrastructure*, for more information; it is available at http://csrc.nist.gov/publications/nistpubs/800-32/sp800-32.pdf.

66 Technical information on IPsec and PKI is available from the working group's Internet-Draft titled *The Internet IP Security PKI Profile of IKEv1/ISAKMP, IKEv2, and PKIX.* The current draft, released in September 2004, is available at http://www.ietf.org/internet-drafts/draft-ietf-pki4ipsec-ikecert-profile-xx.txt.

67 For further information on OCSP, read RFC 2560, *X.509 Internet Public Key Infrastructure Online Certificate Status Protocol – OCSP*, available at http://www.ietf.org/rfc/rfc2560.txt.

68 More information on CRLs is available from RFC 3280, *Internet X.509 Public Key Infrastructure Certificate and Certificate Revocation List (CRL) Profile*, at http://www.ietf.org/rfc/rfc3280.txt.

69 For more information on EAP, see RFC 3748, *Extensible Authentication Protocol (EAP)*, available at http://www.ietf.org/rfc/rfc3748.txt.

(typically an IPsec gateway), a digital signature is used to authenticate the responder to the initiator. One-way authentication, such as one-time passwords or digital certificates on tokens, is well-suited for road warrior usage, while mutual authentication is preferable for environments at high risk of identity spoofing, such as wireless networks.

4.2.3 Cryptography

Setting the cryptography policy involves choosing encryption and integrity protection algorithms and key lengths.[70] Whenever possible, 128-bit AES[71] should be used for the encryption algorithm because of its strength. It is very important to estimate the processing resources that the encryption will require during peak usage. The central processing unit (CPU) is typically the hardware component most affected by encryption. In some cases, a hardware-based encryption engine with customized CPUs, also known as a *cryptographic accelerator*, may be needed for greater throughput, but this may limit the algorithm options. In other cases, IPsec hardware may not be capable of providing sufficient performance when more resource-intensive encryption algorithms (e.g., AES, 3DES) are in use. Another potential issue is export restrictions involving the use of encryption algorithms in certain countries.[72] Also, not all IPsec components may provide support for a particular algorithm.

For integrity checking, most IPsec implementations offer the HMAC-MD5 and HMAC-SHA-1 hashing algorithms. Neither of these algorithms is computationally intensive. Although both plain MD5 and plain SHA-1 have known weaknesses, both are still considered sufficiently secure in their HMAC versions.[73]

In some implementations of IPsec, the cryptography policy settings are not immediately apparent to administrators. The default settings for encryption and integrity protection, as well as the details of each setting, are often located down several levels of menus or are split among multiple locations. It is also challenging with some implementations to alter the settings once they have been located. For example, by having portions of the settings in multiple locations, administrators may need to go back and forth between different configuration screens to ensure that the settings are correct and consistent.

4.2.4 Packet Filter

The purpose of the packet filter is to specify how each type of incoming and outgoing traffic should be handled—whether the traffic should be permitted or denied (usually based on IP addresses, protocols, and ports), and how permitted traffic should be protected (if at all). By default, IPsec implementations typically provide protection for all traffic. In some cases, this may not be advisable because of performance reasons. Encrypting traffic that does not need protection or is already protected (e.g., encrypted by another application) can be a significant waste of resources. For such traffic, the packet filter could specify the use of the null encryption algorithm for ESP, which would provide integrity checks and anti-replay protection, or the packet filter could simply pass along the traffic without any additional protection. One caveat is that the more complex the packet filter becomes, the more likely it is that a configuration error may occur, which could permit traffic to traverse networks without sufficient protection.

---

70 As described in Section 2.2, Federal agencies should use only FIPS-validated algorithms.

71 For more information, read FIPS PUB 197, *Advanced Encryption Standard (AES)*, which is available at http://csrc.nist.gov/publications/fips/fips197/fips-197.pdf.

72 More information on export restrictions is available from the Bureau of Industry and Security, U.S. Department of Commerce, at http://www.access.gpo.gov/bis/index html.

73 For use in digital signatures, NIST has announced that Federal agencies should plan on transitioning from SHA-1 to stronger forms of SHA (e.g., SHA-224, SHA-256) by 2010. This does not affect the use of HMAC-SHA-1 for integrity protection. For more information, see NIST comments from August 2004 posted at http://csrc.nist.gov/hash standards comments.pdf.

An issue related to packet filters is that certain types of traffic are incompatible with IPsec. For example, IPsec cannot negotiate security for multicast and broadcast traffic.[74] This means that some types of applications, such as multicast-based video conferencing, may not be compatible with IPsec. Attempting to use IPsec to secure such traffic often causes communication problems or impairs or breaks application functionality. Other traffic such as Windows browser broadcast requests should not be forwarded to other networks if they have no meaning or relevance on the remote network. Also, ICMP messages generally should not be encrypted (particularly in tunnel mode). For example, ICMP error messages are often generated by an intermediate host such as a router, not a tunnel endpoint; because the source IP address of the error message is the intermediate host's, the receiving host's IPsec policy may not know how to handle the message.[75] Packet filters should be configured not to apply IPsec protection to types of traffic that are incompatible with IPsec—to let the traffic pass through unprotected if that does not compromise security. If the IPsec gateway cannot block broadcasts and other traffic that should not be passed through it, it may also be effective to configure firewalls or routers near the IPsec gateway to block the traffic.

4.2.5 Other Design Considerations

A particularly important consideration in design decisions is the identification and implementation of other security controls. Organizations should have other security controls in place that support and complement the IPsec implementation. For example, organizations should configure packet filtering devices (e.g., firewalls, routers) to restrict direct access to IPsec gateways. Organizations should have policies in place regarding acceptable usage of IPsec connections and software. Organizations may also set minimum security standards for IPsec endpoints, such as mandatory host hardening measures and patch levels; and specify security controls that must be employed by every endpoint, such as host-based personal firewalls,[76] antivirus software, and spyware detection and removal utilities on IPsec client hosts.[77]

For endpoints outside the organization's control, such as systems belonging to business partners, users' home computers, and Internet kiosks, organizations should recognize that some of the endpoints might violate the organization's minimum security standards. For example, some of these external endpoints might be compromised by malware and other threats occasionally; malicious activity could then enter the organization's networks from the endpoints through their IPsec connections. To minimize risk, organizations should restrict the access provided to external endpoints as much as possible, and also ensure that policies, processes, and technologies are in place to detect and respond to suspicious activity. Organizations should be prepared to identify users or endpoint devices of interest and disable their IPsec access rapidly as needed.

IPsec packet filters can be helpful in limiting external IPsec endpoints' access to the organization. Using packet filters to limit acceptable traffic to the minimum necessary for untrusted hosts, along with other network security measures (e.g., firewall rulesets, router access control lists), should be effective in preventing certain types of malicious activity from reaching their targets. Administrators may also need to suspend access temporarily for infected hosts until appropriate host security measures (e.g., antivirus software update, patch deployment) have resolved the infection-related issues. Another option in some

---

74 Section 7.2 contains information on current research efforts to create IPsec solutions for multicast traffic.

75 Some IPsec implementations perform state tracking to determine where ICMP error messages should be sent. Also, the proposed IKEv2, ESPv3, and AHv3 standards have more flexible solutions for handling ICMP messages.

76 Host-based firewalls, also known as personal firewalls, can be very effective at preventing unauthorized access to IPsec endpoints if configured to block unwanted activity. Host-based firewalls might need to be reconfigured from their typical settings to permit legitimate IPsec-related activity. Accordingly, organizations should consider providing information to external endpoint administrators and users on which services, protocols, or port numbers the host-based firewalls should permit for IPsec.

77 DISA's *Secure Remote Computing STIG*, found at http://csrc.nist.gov/pcig/STIGs/src-stig-v1r2.pdf, has an appendix that contains a sample checklist of security controls to be verified on VPN users' systems.

environments is automatically quarantining each remote host that establishes an IPsec connection, checking its host security control settings, and then deciding if it should be permitted to use the organization's networks and resources. It is advisable to perform these checks not only for hosts connecting to the organization's VPN from external locations, but also for mobile systems connecting to the organization's internal network that are also sometimes connected to external networks.

In addition to endpoint security, there are many other possible design considerations. The following items describe specific IPsec settings not addressed earlier in this section:

- **SA Lifetimes.** The IPsec endpoints should be configured to request IKE and IPsec SA lifetimes that balance security and overhead.[78] In general, shorter SA lifetimes tend to support better security, but every SA creation involves additional overhead. Also, the appropriate lifetime is somewhat dependent on the authentication method—for example, a short lifetime may be disruptive to users in a host-to-gateway model that requires users to authenticate manually, but not disruptive in a gateway-to-gateway model with automatic authentication. During testing, administrators should set short lifetimes (perhaps 5 to 10 minutes) so that the rekeying process can be tested more quickly. In operational implementations, IPsec SA lifetimes should generally be set to a few hours, with IKE SA lifetimes set somewhat higher. A common default setting for IKE SAs is a lifetime of 24 hours (86400 seconds), and for IPsec SAs a lifetime of 8 hours (28800 seconds). It is important to ensure that the peers are configured with compatible lifetimes; some implementations will terminate an IKE negotiation if the peer proposes a longer lifetime than its configured value.

- **IKE Phase One Exchange Mode.** As described in Section 3.3.1, main mode should be specified whenever possible because it provides stronger security than aggressive mode.

- **Diffie-Hellman Group Number.** Section 3.3.1.1 lists the standard Diffie-Hellman group definitions. Most products support group 2 (MODP generator, 1024-bit modulus), which provides stronger protection than group 1, so the use of group 1 is not recommended. The Diffie-Hellman (DH) group used to establish the secret keying material for IKE and IPsec should be consistent with current security requirements for the strength of the encryption keys that it is used to generate. For the foreseeable future, DH group 2 (1024-bit MODP) provides sufficient security for both Triple DES and AES with a 128-bit key. For greater security, DH group 5 (1536-bit MODP) or DH group 14 (2048-bit MODP)[79] may be used for AES.[80] The larger DH groups will result in increased processing time.

- **Extra Padding.** As described in Section 3.2.3, ESP packets can contain optional padding that alters the size of the packet to conceal how many bytes of actual data the packet contains, which is helpful in deterring traffic analysis. Having larger packets increases bandwidth usage and the endpoints' processing load for encrypting and decrypting packets, so organizations should only use extra padding if traffic analysis is a significant threat. (In most cases, it is not.)

- **Perfect Forward Secrecy.** Because the Perfect Forward Secrecy option provides stronger security, it can be used if it does not cause excessive overhead or interoperability issues. Generally, PFS should not be enabled during initial IPsec testing; once the basic IPsec implementation is functioning properly, PFS can then be enabled and tested if deemed advisable.

---

78 In most cases, lifetimes should be specified by both time and bytes of traffic so that all SAs, regardless of the volume of traffic, have a limited lifetime. Organizations should not specify a lifetime by bytes of traffic only because an SA that is not used or used lightly might exist indefinitely.

79 NIST recommends upgrading to 2048-bit Diffie-Hellman by 2011.

80 As of mid-2005, all IPsec implementations include DH group 2, most include DH group 5, and very few include DH group 14.

Design decisions should incorporate several other considerations, as described below:

- **Current and Future Network Characteristics.** This document has already described issues involving the use of NAT. Organizations should also be mindful of other network characteristics, such as the use of IPv6 and wireless networking, when designing an IPsec implementation. For example, if the organization is planning on deploying IPv6 technologies in the near future, it may be desirable to deploy an IPsec solution that already supports IPv6.
- **Incident Response.** Organizations should consider how IPsec components may be affected by incidents and create a design that supports effective and efficient incident response activities. For example, if an IPsec user's system is compromised, this should necessitate canceling existing credentials used for IPsec authentication, such as revoking a digital certificate or deleting a pre-shared key.
- **Log Management.** IPsec should be configured so that it logs sufficient details regarding successful and failed IPsec connection attempts to support troubleshooting and incident response activities. IPsec logging should adhere to the organization's policies on log management, such as requiring copies of all log entries to be sent through a secure mechanism to centralized log servers, and preserving IPsec gateway log entries for a certain number of days.
- **Redundancy.** Organizations should carefully consider the need for a robust IPsec solution that can survive the failure of one or more components. If IPsec is supporting critical functions within the organization, then the IPsec implementation should probably have some duplicate or redundant components. For example, an organization could have two IPsec gateways configured so that when one gateway fails, users automatically fail over to the other gateway (assuming that the gateways support such a failover capability). Redundancy and failover capabilities should be considered not only for the core IPsec components, but also for supporting systems such as authentication servers and directory servers.

4.2.6 Summary of Design Decisions

Table 4-1 provides a checklist that summarizes the major design decisions made during the first two phases of the IPsec planning and implementation process.

Table 4-1. Design Decisions Checklist

Completed	Design Decision
Identify Needs	
	Determine which communications need to be protected
	Determine what protective measures are needed for each type of communication
	Identify other current and future requirements
	Consider the possible technical solutions and select the one that best meets the identified needs
Design the Solution—Architecture	
	Determine where IPsec hosts and gateways should be located within the network architecture
	Select appropriate IPsec client software for hosts
	Determine whether split tunneling should be permitted
	Determine whether IPsec hosts should be issued virtual IP addresses
Design the Solution—Authentication	
	Decide which authentication methods should be supported
	Identify methods to perform key management for authentication credentials
Design the Solution—Cryptography	
	Choose encryption and integrity protection algorithms and key lengths
Design the Solution—Packet Filter	
	Determine which types of traffic should be permitted and denied
	Determine what protection and compression measures (if any) should be applied to each type of permitted traffic
Design the Solution—Other Design Considerations	
	Select maximum lifetimes for IKE and IPsec SAs
	Choose main or aggressive mode for the IKE phase one exchange
	Select an appropriate Diffie-Hellman group number for each chosen encryption algorithm and key size
	Determine whether extra padding should be used to thwart traffic analysis
	Decide whether PFS should be enabled

4.3 Implement and Test Prototype

After the solution has been designed, the next step is to implement and test a prototype of the design. This could be done in one or more environments, including a lab network, a test network, and a production network.[81] Aspects of the solution to evaluate include the following:

- **Connectivity.** Users can establish and maintain connections that use IPsec for all types of traffic that are intended to be protected by IPsec, and cannot establish connections for traffic that IPsec is intended to block. It is important to verify that all of the protocols that need to flow through the connection can do so. This should be tested after initial SA negotiation as well as after the original SAs have expired and new SAs have been negotiated. (During testing, it may be helpful to temporarily shorten the SA lifetimes so that renegotiation occurs more quickly.) Connectivity testing should also evaluate possible fragmentation-related issues (e.g., certificates).

[81] Ideally, implementation and testing should first be performed with a lab network, then a test network. Only implementations in final testing should be placed onto a production network. The nature of IPsec allows a phased introduction on the production network as well.

- **Protection.** Each traffic flow should be protected in accordance with the information gathered during the Identify Needs phase. This should be verified by monitoring network traffic and checking IPsec endpoint logs to confirm that the packet filter rules are ensuring the proper protection is provided for each type of traffic.

- **Authentication.** Performing robust testing of authentication is important because if authentication services are lost, IPsec services may be lost as well. Authentication solutions such as digital signatures may be complex and could fail in various ways. See Section 4.2.2 for more information on authentication.

- **Application Compatibility.** The solution should not break or interfere with the use of existing software applications. This includes network communications between application components, as well as IPsec client software issues (e.g., conflict with host-based firewall or intrusion detection software).

- **Management.** Administrators should be able to configure and manage the solution effectively and securely. This includes all components, including gateways, management servers, and client software. For host-to-gateway architectures, it is particularly important to evaluate the ease of deployment and configuration. For example, most implementations do not have fully automated client configuration; in many cases, administrators manually configure each client. Another concern is the ability of users to alter IPsec settings, causing connections to fail and requiring administrators to manually reconfigure the client, or causing a security breach.

- **Logging.** The logging and data management functions should function properly in accordance with the organization's policies and strategies.

- **Performance.** The solution should be able to provide adequate performance during normal and peak usage. Performance issues are among the most common IPsec-related problems. It is important to consider not only the performance of the primary IPsec components, but also that of intermediate devices, such as routers and firewalls. Encrypted traffic often consumes more processing power than unencrypted traffic, so it may cause bottlenecks.[82] Also, because IPsec headers and tunneling increase the packet length, intermediate network devices might need to fragment them, possibly slowing network activity.[83] In many cases, the best way to test the performance under load of a prototype implementation is to use simulated traffic generators on a live test network to mimic the actual characteristics of expected traffic as closely as possible. Testing should incorporate a variety of applications that will be used with IPsec, especially those that are most likely to be affected by network throughput or latency issues, such as Voice Over IP.[84] Addressing performance problems generally involves upgrading or replacing hardware, offloading cryptographic calculations from software to specialized hardware, or reducing processing needs (e.g., using a more efficient encryption algorithm, only encrypting sensitive traffic).

- **Security of the Implementation.** The IPsec implementation itself may contain vulnerabilities and weaknesses that attackers could exploit. Organizations with high security needs may want to perform extensive vulnerability assessments against the IPsec components. At a minimum, the

---

82 The additional resources necessitated by IPsec vary widely based on several factors, including the IPsec mode (tunnel or transport), the encryption algorithm, and the use of IPComp, UDP encapsulation, or optional padding.

83 Similar problems can occur when tunnels are within other tunnels, so that packets are encapsulated multiple times. Typically, the solution for these types of problems is to reduce the size of the maximum transmission unit (MTU) value on the host originating the network traffic. The MTU is the maximum allowable packet size. The MTU can be lowered so that the IPsec-encapsulated packets are not large enough to require fragmentation.

84 For more information on Voice Over IP, see NIST SP 800-58, *Security Considerations for Voice Over IP Systems*, available at http://csrc.nist.gov/publications/nistpubs/index.html.

testers should update all components with the latest patches and configure the components following sound security practices. Section 4.3.2 presents some common IPsec security concerns.

- **Component Interoperability.** The components of the IPsec solution must function together properly. This is of greatest concern when a variety of components from different vendors may be used. Section 4.3.1 contains more information on interoperability concerns.
- **Default Settings.** Besides the IPsec settings described in Section 4.2, IPsec implementations may have other configuration settings. IPsec implementers should carefully review the default values for each setting and alter the settings as necessary to support their design goals. They should also ensure that the implementation does not unexpectedly "drop back" to default settings for interoperability or other reasons.

4.3.1 Component Interoperability

Another facet of testing to consider is the compatibility and interoperability of the IPsec components. Although there has been improvement in the industry, IPsec implementations have historically faced the challenge of interoperating between various vendors and implementations. Because many vendors offer IPsec clients and gateways, implementation differences among products can lead to interoperability problems. Although IPsec vendors use the term "IPsec compliant" to state that they meet the current IETF IPsec standards, they may implement the standards differently, which can cause subtle and hard-to-diagnose problems. Also, some products provide support for components (e.g., encryption algorithms) that are not part of the IPsec standards; this is done for various reasons, including enhancing ease of use, providing additional functionality, and addressing weak or missing parts of the standards. Examples of compatibility issues are as follows:

- The endpoints support different encryption algorithms, compression algorithms, or authentication methods.
- One endpoint requires the usage of a proprietary feature for proper operation.
- The endpoints may encode or interpret certain digital certificate fields or data differently.
- The endpoints default to different parameters, such as Diffie-Hellman group 2 versus group 1.
- The endpoints implement different interpretations of ambiguous or vaguely worded standards, such as performing SA rekeying in different ways.
- Most gateway implementations interoperate with other vendors' implementations, but many client implementations only interoperate with their own vendor's gateway implementation.

The following are some IKE-related interoperability issues:

- **Certificate Contents.** Different implementations may encode or interpret certificate data fields (e.g., peer identity) differently, or handle certificate extensions in conflicting ways.
- **Rekeying Behavior.** When implementations re-negotiate IKE or IPsec SAs, different rekeying behavior can result in lost traffic. One potential area of difficulty is timing-related: when to start using the new SA and when to delete the old SA. In addition, when an IKE SA expires, some implementations delete all IPsec SAs that were negotiated using that IKE SA. Other implementations allow the IPsec SAs to continue until they, in turn, expire. This can also cause interoperability problems.

- **Initial Contact Messages.** Some implementations send an Initial Contact notification message when they begin an IKE negotiation with a peer for whom they have no current SAs. This can also be an indication that the sending implementation has rebooted and lost previously negotiated SAs. There can be incompatibility issues if one implementation sends and expects to receive this message, and the other one has not implemented this feature.

- **Dead Peer Detection (DPD).** Dead peer detection enables an endpoint to ensure that its peer is still able to communicate. This can help the endpoint to avoid a situation in which it expends processing resources to send IPsec-protected traffic to a peer that is no longer available. If no traffic is sent through an SA, some implementations will delete the SA, even if the negotiated lifetime has not elapsed. DPD messages can be sent to ensure that an otherwise unused SA is kept alive. This can avoid NAT mapping timeouts or deletion of inactive SAs.

- **Vendor ID.** One endpoint may depend upon a Vendor ID feature that is either absent or inconsistently implemented by the peer.

- **Lifetimes.** Peers may be configured with different values for IKE or IPsec SA lifetimes.

The best way to determine interoperability between vendors is to actually test them in a lab environment. Another approach is to research issues with the products by using Web sites that provide interoperability testing configuration and results, as well as the ability to perform real-time testing. The following are sources of testing or interoperability information:

- The NIST IP Security Web Based Interoperability Tester (IPsec-WIT)[85] offers real-time IPsec interoperability testing. It provides the ability to test an IPsec implementation with the reference IPsec implementation at NIST. Testers can choose to negotiate a security association with the NIST implementation through IKE or to establish an SA manually with the NIST implementation.

- Another source of information on IPsec compatibility is the ICSA Labs Web site.[86] In 1998, ICSA Labs addressed vendor interoperability issues by establishing the IPsec Product Developers Consortium and the IPsec Product Certification Testing Program with interoperability as the primary focus. The ICSA Labs Web site lists in detail the parameters that are tested and the products that are certified against each set of criteria.[87]

- The Virtual Private Network Consortium (VPNC) is a trade association for VPN vendors.[88] One of the goals of the VPNC is to improve interoperability among products. It offers interoperability tests and certifies products as being interoperable with many others. According to the VPNC Web site, "a system has to interoperate with at least three quarters of the other systems that are in the test" to receive Basic Interoperability certification. "Interoperability is defined as creating a working IKE tunnel…[which] requires Triple DES for encryption, SHA-1 for hash, 1024-bit key exchange, and a preshared secret for authentication." VPNC offers a separate certification for products using 128-bit AES encryption.[89]

85 More information on the NIST IP Security Web Based Interoperability Tester is available at http://ipsec-wit.antd.nist.gov/.
86 The ICSA Lab Web site is located at https://www.icsalabs.com/ipsec.
87 ICSA offers a document titled *IPsec Product Technical Configuration Guidelines* that addresses configuration parameters and practices to use for interoperability testing. The document is available at http://www.icsalabs.com/icsa/docs/html/communities/ipsec/IPsec_Technical_Config_Guidelines.pdf.
88 The VPNC Web site is located at http://www.vpnc.org/.
89 The VPNC Testing for Interoperability Web page is located at http://www.vpnc.org/testing.html.

- Many IPsec vendors have also performed their own interoperability testing and made the results public on their Web sites so that their products can be configured to operate with other common products. Most vendors also offer configuration guidelines and notes to facilitate interoperability.

4.3.2 Security of the Implementation

Another topic to keep in mind during testing is the security of the IPsec implementation itself. IPsec was built with careful thought and consideration for security; however, no protocol or software is completely bulletproof. Security concerns regarding IPsec include the following:

- Some IPsec implementations store the pre-shared keys in plain text on the system. This can be accessed by legitimate users and anyone else who gains access to the system. The use of such implementations should be avoided if unauthorized physical access to the system is a concern. However, if it is necessary to use such a product, be sure to apply the appropriate system hardening measures and deploy host-based firewalls and intrusion detection software.

- IPsec allows some traffic to pass unprotected, such as broadcast, multicast, IKE, and Kerberos. Attackers could potentially use this knowledge to their advantage to send unauthorized malicious traffic through the IPsec filters. Be sure to carefully monitor the traffic that is passing through the IPsec tunnel, as well as that which is bypassing it. For example, network-based intrusion detection system (IDS) or intrusion prevention system (IPS) devices can typically be configured to alert on non-tunneled traffic.

- Periodically, vulnerabilities are discovered in IPsec implementations. Organizations such as US-CERT notify vendors of new vulnerabilities and, at the appropriate time, also notify the public of the issues and the recommended resolutions, such as installing vendor-supplied patches. Information on known vulnerabilities is provided by various online databases, including the National Vulnerability Database (NVD).[90]

4.4 Deploy the Solution

Once testing is complete and any issues have been resolved, the next phase of the IPsec planning and implementation model involves deploying the solution. A prudent strategy is to gradually migrate existing network infrastructure, applications, and users to the new IPsec solution. The phased deployment provides administrators an opportunity to evaluate the impact of the IPsec solution and resolve issues prior to enterprise wide deployment. Most of the issues that can occur during IPsec deployment are the same types of issues that occur during any large IT deployment. Typical issues that are IPsec-specific are as follows:

- Encrypted traffic can negatively affect services such as firewalls, intrusion detection, Quality of Service (QoS), remote monitoring (RMON) probes, and congestion control protocols.

- Unexpected performance issues may arise, either with the IPsec components themselves (e.g., gateways) or with intermediate devices, such as routers.

- IPsec may not work properly on some production networks because of firewalls, routers, and other intermediate packet filtering devices that block IPsec traffic. For example, the devices might have been misconfigured for IPsec traffic or not configured at all—for example, if the IPsec implementers were not aware of the existence of a device. Misconfigured devices are more likely to be an issue with organizations that use a wider variety of network devices or have

---

[90] The US-CERT Web site is located at http://www.us-cert.gov/. The NVD Web site is located at http://nvd.nist.gov/.

decentralized network device administration and management. In such environments, the changes needed to permit IPsec could vary widely among devices.

- The environment may change during the deployment. For example, IPsec client software may be broken by a new operating system update. This issue can be handled rather easily in a managed environment, but it can pose a major problem if users have full control over their systems and can select their own client software.

4.5 Manage the Solution

The last phase of the IPsec planning and implementation model is the longest lasting. Managing the solution involves maintaining the IPsec architecture, policies, software, and other components of the deployed solution. Examples of typical maintenance actions are testing and applying patches to IPsec software, deploying IPsec to additional remote sites, configuring additional user laptops as IPsec clients, performing key management duties (e.g., issuing new credentials, revoking credentials for compromised systems or departing users) and adapting the policies as requirements change. It is also important to monitor the performance of IPsec components so that potential resource issues can be identified and addressed before components become overwhelmed. Another important task is to perform testing periodically to verify that the IPsec controls are functioning as expected. Any new hardware, software, or significant configuration changes starts the process again at the Identify Needs phase. This ensures that the IPsec solution lifecycle operates effectively and efficiently.

Another aspect of managing the IPsec solution is handling operational issues. For example, a common problem is poor performance caused by undesired fragmentation. When it comes to troubleshooting IPsec connections, a network sniffer such as tcpdump or Ethereal is typically very helpful.[91] A sniffer allows the administrator to analyze the communications as they take place and correct problems. IPsec gateway logs and client logs may also be valuable resources during troubleshooting; firewall and router logs may validate whether the IPsec traffic is reaching them, passing through them, or being blocked. ICSA Labs has written a document titled *IPsec VPN Advanced Troubleshooting Guide*.[92] This document offers suggestions and best practices for troubleshooting IPsec connections, addressing potential problem areas such as fragmentation, firewalls, NAT, and digital certificates.

4.6 Summary

This section has described a phased approach to IPsec planning and implementation and highlighted various issues that may be of significance to implementers. The following summarizes the key points from the section:

- The use of a phased approach for IPsec planning and implementation can help to achieve successful IPsec deployments. The five phases of the approach are as follows:
  1. Identify Needs—Identify the need to protect network communications and determine how that need can best be met.
  2. Design the Solution—Make design decisions in four areas: architectural considerations, authentication methods, cryptography policy, and packet filters.

---

91 tcpdump is available for download at http://sourceforge.net/projects/tcpdump/. Ethereal is available for download from http://www.ethereal.com/.

92 The guide is available at http://www.icsalabs.com/icsa/docs/html/communities/ipsec/IPsec_Advanced_Toubleshooting_GuideFinal.pdf.

3. Implement and Test a Prototype—Test a prototype of the designed solution in a lab or test environment to identify any potential issues.

4. Deploy the Solution—Gradually deploy IPsec throughout the enterprise.

5. Manage the Solution—Maintain the IPsec components and resolve operational issues; repeat the planning and implementation process when significant changes need to be incorporated into the solution.

- The placement of an IPsec gateway has potential security, functionality, and performance implications. Specific factors to consider include device performance, traffic examination, gateway outages, and NAT.
- Although IPsec clients built into operating systems may be more convenient than deploying third-party client software, third-party clients may offer features that built-in clients do not.
- When IPsec hosts are located outside the organization's networks, it may be desirable to assign them virtual internal IP addresses to provide compatibility with existing IP address-based security controls.
- Authentication options include pre-shared keys, digital signatures, and (in some implementations) external authentication services such as Kerberos. An authentication solution should be selected based primarily on maintenance, scalability, and security.
- Cryptographic algorithms and key lengths that are considered secure for current practice should be used for encryption and integrity protection. Triple DES or AES with a 128-bit key are recommended for encryption; HMAC-SHA-1 is recommended for integrity protection.
- Packet filters should apply appropriate protections to traffic and not protect other types of traffic for performance or functionality reasons.
- Specific design decisions include SA lifetimes, IKE phase 1 mode, Diffie-Hellman group number, extra packet padding, and the use of PFS. Additional design considerations include current and future network characteristics, incident response, log management, redundancy, and other security controls already in place.
- Testing of the prototype implementation should evaluate several factors, including connectivity, protection, authentication, application compatibility, management, logging, performance, the security of the implementation, component interoperability, and default settings.
- During full implementation, existing network infrastructure, applications, and users should gradually be migrated to the new IPsec solution. This provides administrators an opportunity to evaluate the impact of the IPsec solution and resolve issues prior to enterprise wide deployment.
- After implementation, the IPsec solution needs to be maintained, such as applying patches and deploying IPsec to additional networks and hosts. Operational issues also need to be addressed and resolved.
- Organizations should implement technical, operational, and management controls that support and complement IPsec implementations. Examples include having control over all entry and exit points for the protected networks, ensuring the security of all IPsec endpoints, and incorporating IPsec considerations into organizational policies.

5. Alternatives to IPsec

Although IPsec is flexible enough to meet many needs, there are certain cases when other protocols may provide a better solution. This section lists several VPN protocols that are used as alternatives to IPsec, and groups them by the layer of the TCP/IP model (as shown in Figure 5-1)[93] at which they function, because many of the protocols' characteristics are based on the layer they use. IPsec is the prevalent network layer VPN protocol; this section discusses several data link layer, transport layer, and application layer VPN protocols. For each protocol, a brief description is provided, along with a description of the circumstances under which it may be more advantageous than IPsec.

Application Layer. This layer sends and receives data for particular applications, such as Domain Name System (DNS), HyperText Transfer Protocol (HTTP), and Simple Mail Transfer Protocol (SMTP).
Transport Layer. This layer provides connection-oriented or connectionless services for transporting application layer services between networks. The transport layer can optionally assure the reliability of communications. Transmission Control Protocol (TCP) and User Datagram Protocol (UDP) are commonly used transport layer protocols.
Network Layer. This layer routes packets across networks. Internet Protocol (IP) is the fundamental network layer protocol for TCP/IP. Other commonly used protocols at the network layer are Internet Control Message Protocol (ICMP) and Internet Group Management Protocol (IGMP).
Data Link Layer. This layer handles communications on the physical network components. The best-known data link layer protocol is Ethernet.

Figure 5-1. TCP/IP Layers

5.1 Data Link Layer VPN Protocols

Data link layer VPN protocols function below the network layer in the TCP/IP model. This means that various network protocols, such as IP, IPX, and NetBEUI, can usually be used with a data link layer VPN. Most VPN protocols (including IPsec) only support IP, so data link layer VPN protocols may provide a viable option for protecting networks running non-IP protocols. (As the name implies, IPsec is designed to provide security for IP traffic only.)

The most commonly implemented data link layer VPN protocols are typically used on top of the Point-to-Point Protocol (PPP)[94] and are most often used to secure modem-based connections. PPP, not the VPN protocol itself, typically provides encryption and authentication services for the traffic. The standards for PPP only reference supporting DES for encryption and PAP (Password Authentication Protocol) and CHAP (Challenge Handshake Authentication Protocol) for authentication.[95] Because there are known weaknesses in these algorithms, data link layer VPN protocols often make use of additional protocols and services to provide stronger encryption and authentication for VPN connections. The most commonly used data link layer VPN protocols are as follows:

---

93 Figure 5-1 repeats Figure 2-1 for additional clarity.

94 For more information on PPP, see RFC 1661, *The Point-to-Point Protocol (PPP)*, available at http://www.ietf.org/rfc/rfc1661.txt.

95 For more information on PPP encryption and authentication, see RFC 1968, *The PPP Encryption Control Protocol (ECP)* (available at http://www.ietf.org/rfc/rfc1968.txt) and RFC 1334, *PPP Authentication Protocols* (available at http://www.ietf.org/rfc/rfc1334.txt).

- **Point-to-Point Tunneling Protocol (PPTP)[96] Version 2**
  - PPTP provides a protected tunnel between a PPTP-enabled client (e.g., a personal computer) and a PPTP-enabled server. Each system that may use PPTP needs to have PPTP client software installed and configured appropriately.
  - PPTP uses IP protocol 47, Generic Routing Encapsulation (GRE), to transport data.[97] Most packet filtering devices block this protocol by default, so they may need to be reconfigured to permit it. In addition to the GRE connection, PPTP also establishes a separate control channel using TCP port 1723.
  - Microsoft has created its own PPP encryption mechanism for use with PPTP, Microsoft Point-to-Point Encryption (MPPE); it uses a 40-bit or 128-bit key with the RSA RC4 algorithm.[98] Microsoft has also created MS-CHAP to provide stronger authentication than PAP and CHAP; however, researchers have found serious weaknesses in MS-CHAP.[99]
  - The original version of PPTP contained serious security flaws. PPTP version 2 addressed many of these issues, but researchers have identified weaknesses with it as well (in addition to the MS-CHAP issues).[100]
- **Layer 2 Tunneling Protocol (L2TP)[101]**
  - Like PPTP, L2TP protects communications between an L2TP-enabled client and an L2TP-enabled server, and it requires L2TP client software to be installed and configured on each user system.
  - Unlike PPTP, which relies on GRE to tunnel data, L2TP uses its own tunneling protocol, which runs over UDP port 1701. Because of this, L2TP may be easier to pass through packet filtering devices than PPTP. Also, L2TP can support multiple sessions within the same tunnel.
  - In addition to the PPP-provided authentication methods, L2TP can also use other methods, such as RADIUS and TACACS+.
  - As described in Section 4, L2TP often uses IPsec to provide encryption and key management services.
- **Layer 2 Forwarding (L2F)[102]**
  - Unlike PPTP and L2TP, L2F is intended for use between network devices, such as an ISP's network access server and an organization's VPN gateway. Users establish unprotected

---

96 For more information on PPTP, see RFC 2637, *Point-to-Point Tunneling Protocol,* available at http://www.ietf.org/rfc/rfc2637.txt.

97 More information on GRE is available in RFC 2784, *Generic Routing Encapsulation (GRE)*, at http://www.ietf.org/rfc/rfc2784.txt.

98 For more information on MPPE, see RFC 3078, *Microsoft Point-to-Point Encryption (MPPE) Protocol*, available at http://www.ietf.org/rfc/rfc3078.txt.

99 One paper discussing MS-CHAP weaknesses is *Exploiting Known Security Holes in Microsoft's PPTP Authentication Extensions (MS-CHAPv2)* by Jochen Eisinger (http://mopo.informatik.uni-freiburg.de/pptp_mschapv2/).

100 For more information on PPTP security issues, see Bruce Schneier's PPTP Web page, located at http://www.schneier.com/pptp.html.

101 For more information on L2TP, see RFC 2661, *Layer Two Tunneling Protocol "L2TP"*, available at http://www.ietf.org/rfc/rfc2661.txt.

102 For more information on L2F, see RFC 2341, *Cisco Layer Two Forwarding (Protocol) "L2F"*, available at http://www.ietf.org/rfc/rfc2341.txt.

connections from their computers to the ISP. The ISP recognizes that the users' traffic should be tunneled to the organization, so it authenticates each user and the organization's VPN gateway, then provides protection for the traffic between the ISP and the organization. The use of L2F requires the ISP's support and participation.

- Because L2F is not client-based, users' systems do not need L2F client software or configuration. However, this also means that communications between the users' systems and the ISP are completely unprotected.
- Like L2TP, L2F can use authentication protocols such as RADIUS and TACACS+. However, L2F does not support encryption.

L2TP was intended to replace PPTP and L2F. When configured properly, L2TP combined with IPsec can provide strong encryption and authentication. PPTP should not be used to protect communications because of its known weaknesses. Because L2F can provide only limited protection for portions of communications that involve a participating ISP, L2TP should typically be used instead of L2F. L2TP with IPsec is a viable option for providing confidentiality and integrity for dial-up communications, particularly for organizations that contract VPN services to an ISP.

Besides protecting dial-up connections, data link layer VPN protocols are also used in high security environments to secure particular physical links, such as a dedicated circuit between two buildings, when there is concern regarding unauthorized physical access to the link's components. The VPN can be established by deploying a gateway that encrypts and decrypts data at each end of the circuit, or by adding VPN services to endpoints such as switches. *Provisioner-provided VPNs* (PPVPN) refer to the link's service provider offering VPN protection for the link. In a PPVPN, the management and maintenance of the VPN are primarily the responsibility of the service provider, not the organizations using the link. The IETF's Layer 2 Virtual Private Networks (L2VPN) working group is currently developing standards for data link layer PPVPNs.[103]

5.2 Transport Layer VPN Protocols

As discussed in Section 2.1, transport layer protocols such as TLS are most commonly used to provide security for communications with individual HTTP-based applications, although they can be used to provide protection for communication sessions for other types of applications as well. Under the traditional transport layer protocol model, each application server that needs its communications protected must include support for the protocol, as must the client portion of each application. Because all major Web browsers include support for TLS, users who wish to use Web-based applications that are protected by TLS normally do not need to install any client software or reconfigure their systems. This technique has been in widespread use since the mid-1990s. One important difference between TLS and IPsec protection is that while IPsec authenticates each endpoint to the other, TLS authentication is typically one-way, authenticating the server to the client. (TLS is also capable of authenticating the client to the server as well, but in practice, most TLS implementations do not take advantage of this feature.)

A more recent development is the use of TLS reverse proxy servers (commonly referred to as *SSL proxy servers, TLS VPNs*, and *SSL VPNs*) to provide a more robust VPN solution for remote users.[104] A remote

---

[103] More information on the L2VPN working group is available at http://www.ietf.org/html.charters/l2vpn-charter.html. PPVPNs are also available at the network layer; the primary motivation is to provide a VPN solution that can support additional services besides encryption and authentication, such as traffic management and service differentiation. The Layer 3 VPN (L3VPN) working group is developing standards for network layer PPVPNs; their home page is located at http://www.ietf.org/html.charters/l3vpn-charter.html.

[104] Although this discussion assumes that TLS proxy servers provide transport layer VPN services, proxy server vendors label them as network layer, transport layer, or application layer VPNs. This is largely dependent upon the features that the server provides; for example, some transport layer servers have been extended to issue IP addresses to clients, which is a network

user who needs to use some of the organization's applications enters the main Uniform Resource Locator (URL) for the proxy server in a Web browser and connects to it through TLS-protected HTTP.[105] The user then provides authentication to the proxy server. Once authenticated, the user can then access designated applications, as specified in the proxy server's access controls. The user does not access the applications directly; the user's system has a TLS-protected HTTP connection with the proxy server. The proxy server then establishes another connection between itself and the application server; this connection is protected or unprotected as appropriate.

To allow users from outside the organization's network to access Web-based internal applications, the TLS VPN often has to re-write URLs that appear in the organization's internal Web pages. These URLs can take numerous forms, including links to internal private addresses, links generated by programs such as JavaScript or Flash, and links that incorporate addresses in non-standard formats. The VPN Consortium tests TLS VPNs to ensure that they correctly handle this challenge, as well as other common uses of TLS VPNs.[106]

Although the TLS proxy server method is well-suited to protecting Web-based applications, it is unable to handle non-Web-based applications in the same manner. Some TLS VPN products provide support for non-Web-based applications (including UDP-based applications) by deploying a special client program (often a Web browser applet, plug-in, or other control) to each user's machine and then tunneling the applications over HTTPS (secure HTTP) or another protocol. Another approach is to set up a terminal server within the organization that contains the actual client software for the non-Web-based applications that need to be accessed remotely. System administrators or users must then install a Web-based terminal server client onto each system that needs to use any of the applications. The Web-based connection to the terminal server is protected by the proxy server just as any other HTTP application would be.

Potential advantages of the proxy server method include the following:

- If access is needed to only Web-based applications, the solution is very convenient for users and easier to deploy and maintain than remote access solutions that involve client installation or configuration.
- The proxy server can authenticate users before they can gain any access to applications, as opposed to allowing users to connect to individual applications' login screens. This adds another layer of security by only allowing authenticated users to see what applications are being served.
- Users cannot directly connect to the application servers; this provides better protection for the application servers against reconnaissance and attacks.
- Since the client systems connect above the network layer, they are not on the network in the same manner that IPsec client systems would be. This severely reduces their ability to attack or misuse systems on the organization's networks.
- Because the proxy server is managing application access for each user, it typically provides granular access controls that can limit which applications each user can access. The proxy server

---

layer service. Proxy servers providing network layer VPN services lose many of the advantages of transport layer VPNs because they typically require client software to be installed to allow client systems to join the organization's network. Differentiating between transport and application layer VPNs is mainly dependent on the number of applications that the VPN protects (multiple applications and a single application, respectively).

105 A TLS-protected HTTP connection is commonly referred to as an HTTPS connection. For more information on this, see RFC 2818, *HTTP Over TLS*, available at http://www.ietf.org/rfc/rfc2818.txt.

106 More information is available from the VPN Consortium Web site at http://www.vpnc.org/testing.html.

also usually has robust logging capabilities that can track authentication attempts and application usage for each user.

- The use of HTTPS makes the proxy server architecture fully compatible with NAT. HTTPS usage is also typically already permitted by firewall rulesets.
- Protection may only be needed for communications over the Internet. In that case, the application servers do not need to provide protection, reducing the resource usage associated with encryption and decryption.

The proxy server method also has some drawbacks, as follows:

- Non-web-based applications and applications that are more challenging to proxy (e.g., those that use multiple dynamic ports) typically require additional software and services, such as terminal servers and special client software. This makes the solution more resource-intensive to deploy and less convenient to use.
- As discussed in Section 2.1, transport layer controls cannot provide any protection for network layer information, such as IP addresses.
- A compromise of the proxy server could allow an attacker to intercept data and authentication credentials for many different applications at once.

The proxy server method is best suited to providing protection for a sizable number of Web-based applications. If users need to access only a few Web-based applications, the proxy server method may not provide a substantial benefit over protecting applications individually with TLS, given the proxy server method's higher overhead and resource requirements. If users need access to many non-Web-based applications, the proxy server method may not provide any benefit over IPsec. In addition, IPsec can protect IP characteristics, which the proxy server method cannot. When considering a TLS proxy server solution, organizations should carefully consider current and future application usage needs, in addition to security-related requirements.

5.3 Application Layer VPN Protocols

As discussed in Section 2.1, each application layer protocol provides protection for only a single application. In many cases, the protocol protects only a portion of the application data. For example, encryption programs such as PGP[107] and GnuPG (GPG)[108] can be used in conjunction with an e-mail client to encrypt the body of an e-mail, but not the e-mail headers (which include addressing information). Application layer VPN protocols could also be built into applications to provide protection for data without requiring the usage of separate applications. Generally, if off-the-shelf software does not already include application layer protection, protection can only be added through another product (either at the application layer or another layer)—for example, wrapping an HTTP-based application with TLS, or deploying an IPsec-based VPN.

A commonly used application layer protocol suite is Secure Shell (SSH), which contains secure replacements for several unencrypted application protocols, including telnet, rcp, and FTP.[109] The SSH client program itself provides protection for remote logins to another system. Some organizations extend the use of the SSH application by establishing SSH tunnels between hosts, and then passing other communications through the tunnels. This allows many applications to be protected at one time through a

107 More information on PGP is available at http://www.pgp.com/.
108 More information on GPG is available at http://www.gnupg.org/.
109 For more information on Secure Shell, see http://www.ssh.com/ and http://www.openssh.com/.

single tunnel. Generally, the tunnel is constructed between a remote user's system and a server within the organization that the user can log into. Because a single SSH tunnel can provide protection for several applications at once, it is technically a transport layer VPN protocol, not application layer.

SSH tunnel-based VPNs are resource-intensive to set up. They require the installation and configuration of SSH client software on each user's machine, as well as the reconfiguration of client applications to use the tunnel. Each user must also have login privileges on a server within the organization; because this server typically needs to be directly accessible from the Internet, it is susceptible to attack. Generally, users need to have solid technical skills so that they can configure systems and applications themselves, as well as troubleshoot problems that occur. The most common users of SSH tunnel-based VPNs are small groups of IT administrators.

5.4 Summary

Section 5 describes the main alternatives to IPsec. Data link layer VPN protocols, such as PPTP, L2TP, and L2F; transport layer VPN protocols, primarily TLS/SSL; and application layer VPN protocols, including PGP and SSH, are all effective alternatives to IPsec for particular needs and environments. Table 5-1 provides a high-level comparison of the alternatives. The following summarizes the key points from Section 5:

- **Data link layer VPNs** can protect various network protocols, so they are often used for non-IP protocols. One type of data link layer VPN is a provisioner-provided VPN, which can protect communications on a dedicated physical link. Data link layer VPNs are most commonly used on top of PPP to secure modem-based connections, although PPP actually encrypts the traffic.
  - **PPTP** protects communications between a PPTP-enabled client and a PPTP-enabled server, and uses GRE to transport data between them.
  - **L2TP** protects communications between an L2TP-enabled client and an L2TP-enabled server, and uses its own tunneling protocol over UDP port 1701 to transport data.
  - **L2F** protects communications between two network devices, such as ISP network access servers and VPN gateways. It is transparent to users, but it does not protect communications between users' systems and ISPs.
- **Transport layer VPNs** most commonly provide security for communications with individual HTTP-based applications, and can also protect other applications' communications. Each application server must include support for the VPN protocol, as must the client portion of each application. Because all major Web browsers include support for the TLS/SSL protocol, users typically do not need to install client software or reconfigure their systems.
- **TLS/SSL proxy servers** provide network, transport, or application layer VPNs (depending upon the configuration). Typically, remote users connect to the proxy server using TLS-protected HTTP and authenticate themselves; the user can then access designated applications indirectly through the proxy server, which establishes its own separate connections with the application servers. Non-Web-based applications can be accessed by deploying special programs to clients and then tunneling the application data over HTTPS or another protocol; another method is to use a terminal server and to give users a Web-based terminal server client. Unlike IPsec, TLS proxy servers cannot protect IP header characteristics, such as IP addresses.
- **Application layer VPNs** protect part or all of the communications for a single application. For example, e-mail encryption conceals the content in the body of an e-mail, but not the e-mail

headers. Protection is either provided by using a separate program (e.g., a standalone file encryption program) or by building the application layer VPN protocol into the application itself. If neither of these is feasible, a different layer VPN may be needed.

Table 5-1. Comparison of IPsec and IPsec Alternatives

Name	Primary Strengths	Primary Weaknesses	Potential Cases for Use Instead of IPsec
IPsec	+ Already supported by most operating systems + Can provide strong encryption and integrity protection + Transparent to clients in gateway-to-gateway architecture + Can use a variety of authentication protocols	- Can only protect IP-based communications - Requires client software to be configured (and installed on hosts without a built-in client) for host-to-gateway and host-to-host architectures - Does not protect communications between the clients and the IPsec gateway in gateway-to-gateway architectures	N/A
PPTP	+ Can protect non-IP protocols	- Requires client software to be configured (and installed on hosts without a built-in client) - Has known security weaknesses - Does not offer strong authentication - Only supports one session per tunnel	None
L2TP	+ Can protect non-IP protocols + Can support multiple sessions per tunnel + Can use authentication protocols such as RADIUS + Can use IPsec to provide encryption and key management services	- Requires client software to be configured (and installed on hosts without a built-in client)	Protecting dial-up communications
L2F	+ Can protect non-IP protocols + Transparent to clients + Can use authentication protocols such as RADIUS	- Requires each ISP's participation - Does not protect communications between the clients and the ISP - Does not offer encryption; must rely on PPP encryption services, which have known weaknesses	None
SSL/TLS	+ Already supported by all major Web browsers + Can provide strong encryption	- Can only protect TCP-based communications - Requires application servers and clients to support SSL/TLS - Typically implemented to authenticate the server to the client, but not the client to the server	Protecting communications for a small number of HTTP-based applications that do not require strong authentication or provide their own strong authentication mechanism

Name	Primary Strengths	Primary Weaknesses	Potential Cases for Use Instead of IPsec
SSL/TLS Proxy Server	+ Already supported by all major Web browsers + Can provide strong encryption + Can provide multiple layers of authentication	- Can only protect TCP-based communications - Requires clients to support SSL/TLS - Does not protect communications between the proxy server and application servers	Protecting communications for a substantial number of HTTP-based applications
Application Layer VPNs	+ Can provide finely-grained protection for application communications	- Can only protect some or all of the communications for a single application - Often cannot be incorporated into off-the-shelf software - Often use proprietary encryption or authentication mechanisms that may have serious weaknesses	Protecting communications for individual applications that are designed to use proven encryption and authentication algorithm implementations

Table 5-2 lists the TCP and UDP port numbers and IP protocols associated with IPsec and the alternative VPN protocols described in Section 5. This information may be helpful in configuring other network security devices, such as firewalls and routers, to permit VPN activity to pass through.

Table 5-2. IP Protocols and TCP/UDP Port Numbers for VPN Protocols

VPN Protocol	IP Protocols
IPsec	50 (Authentication Header, for AH connections) 51 (for Encapsulating Security Payload, for ESP connections) 17 (UDP), port 500 (for Internet Key Exchange, whether or not NAT-Traversal is used) 17 (UDP), port 4500 (for Internet Key Exchange using NAT-Traversal)
PPTP	47 (Generic Routing Encapsulation) 6 (TCP), port 1723
L2TP	17 (UDP), port 1701
L2F	17 (UDP), port 1701
SSL/TLS	6 (TCP), port 443
SSL/TLS Proxy Server	6 (TCP), port 443
Application Layer VPNs	Varies by application

6. Planning and Implementation Case Studies

This section presents three IPsec solution planning and implementation case studies. Each case study begins by describing a real-world security requirement scenario, such as protecting network communications between two offices. The case study then discusses possible solutions for the security requirement, and explains why IPsec was selected over the alternatives. The next section of each case study discusses the design of the solution and includes a simple network diagram that shows the primary components of the solution (e.g., IPsec gateways and hosts, routers, switches). Each case study also provides some details of the implementation of the solution prototype, which include examples of configuring the solution using commonly available equipment and software, based on an implementation performed in a lab or production environment. Each case study ends with a brief discussion that points out noteworthy aspects of the implementation, indicates when another case study model may be more effective, and discusses variants on the case study scenario that might be of interest to readers.

The case studies are not meant to endorse the use of particular products, nor are any products being recommended over other products. Several common products were chosen so that the case studies would demonstrate a variety of solutions. **Organizations and individuals should not replicate and deploy the sample configuration files or entries.** They are intended to illustrate the decisions and actions involved in configuring the solutions, not to be deployed as-is onto systems.

The case studies presented in this section are as follows:

- Protecting communications between two local area networks (remote office, main office)
- Protecting wireless communications in a small office/home office environment
- Protecting communications between remote users (e.g., telecommuters, road warriors) and the main office's network

6.1 Connecting a Remote Office to the Main Office

An organization with a single office location is planning the creation of a small remote office, which includes identifying any needs to protect network communications. To perform various job functions, most users at the remote office will need to access several IT resources located at the main office, including the organization's e-mail, intranet Web server, databases, and file servers, as well as several business applications. Currently, e-mail is the only one of these resources that can be accessed from outside the main office (it is available through the Internet using a Web-based e-mail client). Communications with most of the IT resources will involve transferring sensitive data (such as financial information) between systems. To support its mission, the organization needs to maintain the confidentiality and integrity of the data in a cost-effective manner. (At this time, the need is to protect communications initiated by remote office hosts to the main office network only; in the future, the solution might be extended to protect communications initiated by main office hosts to the remote office network.) The following sections describe how the organization evaluates its options, identifies a viable solution, creates a design, and implements a prototype.

6.1.1 Identifying Needs and Evaluating Options

As described below, the organization considers a few options for providing access from the remote office to IT resources at the main office and protecting the data:

- **Data Link Layer Solution: Leased Line.** The organization could establish a dedicated leased line between the remote office and the main office. This would provide a private communications mechanism for all the network traffic between the offices. (If the organization were concerned about security breaches of the leased line, additional protection measures such as a data link layer VPN protocol could be used to provide another layer of security.) Unfortunately, because the remote office is geographically distant from the main office, a leased line would be prohibitively expensive.

- **Network Layer Solution: Network Layer VPN.** The organization could establish a network layer VPN between the remote office and main office. Connecting the remote office to the Internet and establishing a VPN tunnel over the Internet between the offices could provide access to the resources and protect the communications. The VPN could have a host-to-gateway architecture, which would reduce hardware costs (only one gateway needed) but increase labor costs (deploying and configuring clients on each remote office system). A gateway-to-gateway architecture would increase hardware costs and decrease labor costs; in effect, the VPN would be invisible to users. The two models also differ in terms of authentication. In a gateway-to-gateway VPN, the gateways would authenticate with each other; in a host-to-gateway VPN, each user would need to authenticate before using the VPN. A gateway-to-gateway VPN could also be configured to permit authorized users from the main office to access resources on the remote office's network. Although this is not a current need, it could be in the future.

- **Transport Layer Solution: Web-Based Applications.** The organization could provide Web-based access to all required IT resources. This could be done either by creating or acquiring Web-based clients for each resource, or by deploying a terminal server that provides access to the resource and providing a Web-based terminal server client to employees. All Web-based applications would use the TLS protocol over HTTP (transport layer security controls) to protect the confidentiality and integrity of data and authentication credentials. By connecting the remote office to the Internet and making the Web-based applications available from the Internet, users at the remote office could use the required IT resources, and the communications would be protected. The main office's network perimeter could be configured to permit external access to the resources only from the remote office's IP address range, which would reduce the risk of external parties gaining unauthorized access to the resources. Users would need to be authenticated by the terminal server, the individual applications, or both the server and the applications.

- **Application Layer Solution: Application Modification.** The organization could purchase add-on software and modify existing applications to provide protection for data within each application. However, a brief review of the required IT resources shows that several of them are off-the-shelf applications that cannot be modified and cannot be protected by third-party application add-ons. Even if the applications could be deployed to protect their own communications, the applications would have to be directly accessible by remote users, which would significantly increase their exposure to threats. The organization is also concerned about the effectiveness of application layer controls in protecting data. Application layer controls may also conceal information from network layer security controls such as network-based intrusion detection systems, necessitating the use of additional host-based security controls that can monitor application layer activity. Having separate controls for each application also complicates or precludes centralized enforcement of security policies across multiple applications, as well as centralized authentication (unless each application supports the use of a third-party authentication server.)

The organization considers the network layer and transport layer options to be the most feasible for meeting its remote access needs. The data link layer and application layer solutions are too expensive, compared to the network and transport layer solutions. Further investigation of the transport layer solution determines that it is not possible or practical to provide Web-based interfaces for several of the desired IT resources. For example, some of the desired applications are off-the-shelf products that offer no Web-based client. A terminal server solution could provide access, but this would require users to connect to the terminal server and authenticate before accessing any applications. Also, each host would need the terminal server client to be installed and configured.

After comparing the three remaining solutions (host-to-gateway network layer VPN, gateway-to-gateway network layer VPN, and terminal server transport layer VPN) and considering how each solution would be deployed in the organization's environment, the organization chooses the gateway-to-gateway network layer VPN. Its primary advantages are that it should be relatively easy for the organization to deploy and maintain, and that it will be transparent to users. The organization also expects to be able to configure the Internet routers at the main office and remote office to act as VPN gateways, so no additional hardware will be needed. Also, each office already routes internally generated network traffic designated for another office's network to its Internet router, so routing changes should need to be made only on the Internet routers themselves. Another advantage of the gateway-to-gateway VPN is that in the future, users at the main office could use it to access resources at the remote office. There is no current need for this, but it is likely that as the remote office matures, this may become a necessity.

6.1.2 Designing the Solution

The organization hopes to use its Internet routers as endpoints for the VPN solution. The routers both support IPsec, and IPsec should be able to protect confidentiality and integrity adequately for the organization's needs, so the plan is to configure the routers to provide an IPsec tunnel. Based on the organization's performance requirements, the routers should be able to handle any additional load because they are currently lightly utilized.[110] Figure 6-1 illustrates the planned design for the VPN architecture. The main office and remote office networks are on separate private networks. Each private network is connected to the Internet through a router that provides NAT services. The plan is to establish an IPsec tunnel between the external interfaces of the two routers. Desktop computers on the remote office network will send unencrypted information to the office's Internet router. The router acts as a VPN gateway, encrypting the traffic and forwarding it to the destination router at the main office, which also acts as a VPN gateway. The main office router decrypts the traffic and forwards it to its final destination, such as a file server or e-mail server. Responses from the servers to the desktops are returned through the tunnel between the gateways.

In this scenario, NAT is an important architectural consideration. If possible, the design should keep NAT services out of the IPsec tunnel path to avoid potential NAT-related incompatibilities and to simplify the design. For this implementation, having the routers NAT outgoing packets before applying IPsec protections is a reasonable solution.

After designing the architecture, the network administrators next consider other elements of the design, including the following:

- **Authentication.** Because the VPN is being established between only two routers, a pre-shared key should provide adequate authentication with minimal effort (as compared to alternatives such as digital certificates). The routers will encrypt the pre-shared key in storage to protect it.[111]

---

110 If the load on the routers increases significantly in the future, cryptography accelerator cards possibly could be added to the routers. (Not all routers support the use of such cards.)

111 The stored pre-shared key is encrypted using AES. See http://www.cisco.com/warp/public/707/pre-sh-keys-ios-rtr-cfg.pdf for more information.

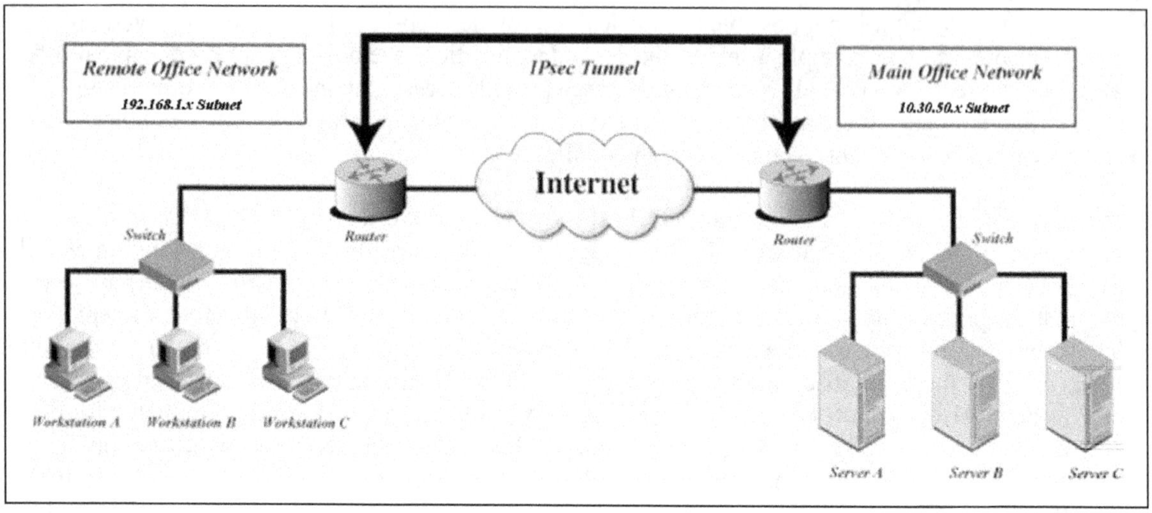

Figure 6-1. Gateway-to-Gateway VPN for Remote Office Connectivity

- **Encryption and Integrity Protection Algorithms.** Although 128-bit AES should provide sufficiently strong encryption, the deployed routers are not capable of supporting AES. However, both routers can support Triple DES, so it is chosen as the encryption algorithm. HMAC-SHA-1 is selected as the integrity protection algorithm because both routers support it and it is the organization's preferred integrity protection algorithm.

- **Packet Filters.** The network administrators work with the security staff to design packet filters that will permit only the necessary network traffic between the two networks and will require adequate protection for traffic. To make initial testing of the solution easier, the administrators decide that the packet filters should allow all IP-based communications from the remote office's hosts to the main office's hosts. Once initial testing has been completed, more restrictive packet filters will be added and tested. The packet filters should permit only the necessary communications and specify the appropriate protection for each type of communication. For example, it might be unnecessary to have IPsec provide protection for traffic generated by accessing the organization's publicly available Web sites.

6.1.3 Implementing a Prototype

Because the organization has limited network equipment and does not have a test lab, the IT staff decides that the best option for validating the solution is to test it after hours using the production routers once the remote office network infrastructure is in place and Internet connectivity has been established. If the testing causes a connectivity outage, the impact should be minimal. The network administrators perform the following steps to configure and test a prototype of the IPsec solution:

1. **Verify the security of the routers.** The network administrators should perform a vulnerability assessment to identify any existing security issues with the routers, such as unneeded user accounts or inadequate physical security controls. The administrators should then address all identified issues before proceeding, or the IPsec implementation may be compromised quickly.

2. **Back up the routers.** Backing up the router operating system and configuration files is a necessity since the prototype is being implemented on production equipment. Even in a test

environment, performing a backup before making any changes is often very helpful because the routers can be restored quickly to a "clean" state.

3. **Update the endpoints to support IPsec.** This could involve updating or patching the operating system, installing or enabling IPsec services, or making other changes to the endpoints so that they can support IPsec services. In this case, both endpoints happen to be Cisco routers, so the administrators double-check each router to confirm that it can support IPsec and the desired encryption algorithm.[112]

4. **Configure authentication.** In this case, each router needs to be configured to use a pre-shared key, as illustrated by the following configuration entries.[113]

   crypto isakmp policy 1[114]
   authentication pre-share
   group 2[115]
   crypto isakmp key *sharedkey* address *xx.xx.xx.xx*[116]

5. **Specify the IPsec mode and cryptographic algorithms.** The following configuration entry on each router specifies ESP tunnel mode, Triple DES encryption, and HMAC-SHA-1 integrity protection:

   crypto ipsec transform-set *auth2* esp-3des esp-sha-hmac[117]

6. **Define the packet filters.** The following configuration entry tells the routers which packets should be permitted to use IPsec:

   access-list *133* permit ip 192.168.1.0 0.0.0.255 10.30.50.0 0.0.0.255

7. **Tie the IPsec settings together in a crypto map.** On Cisco routers, the settings created in steps 2, 3, and 4 need to be connected. This can be done through the following configuration settings, which create a crypto map called *test*:

   crypto map *test* 10 ipsec-isakmp
   set transform-set *auth2*

---

112 IPsec is available with Cisco IOS Software Release 11.3T and later. Because different IOS versions have varying flash memory and RAM requirements, it may be necessary to upgrade the flash memory or RAM before updating the IOS to a version that supports IPsec. Memory requirements for running 3DES and AES vary depending on the router model, IOS version, and feature sets. Individuals with a username and password for Cisco's Web site can look up the minimum DRAM requirements for various routers. Routers may also need to be updated to support for encryption; for example, the IP Plus IPsec 3DES feature pack needs to be installed if Triple DES encryption will be used.

113 Secure transport for the pre-shared key is provided by one of the network administrators, who physically carries a copy of the key from the main office to the remote office.

114 The number 1 represents the priority of the policy.

115 This value is the Diffie-Hellman group identifier.

116 Each router should use the same pre-shared key value for *sharedkey*. Current versions of Cisco IOS store the key in an encrypted format, so that individuals who view the router configuration cannot see the pre-shared key. Also, the plaintext key does not appear in router logs. The argument *xx.xx.xx.xx* should list the IP address of the other router's external interface, so the argument should be different on each router.

117 The term *transform set* refers to the VPN algorithms and security protocols. In this case, auth2 is the name chosen to identify the transform set.

match address *133*
set peer *xx.xx.xx.xx*[118]

8. **Apply the IPsec settings to the external interface.** Because the external interface of the router will provide IPsec services, the crypto map created in the previous step must be applied to the external interface. This is done through the following commands:

   interface FastEthernet0/0
   crypto map *test*

9. **Review the configuration.** After configuring both routers, the administrators review the routers' configurations to ensure that all the necessary settings are in place.[119] The following commands can be used to display the policies:

   show crypto isakmp policy
   show crypto map

10. **Test the solution.** Administrators can test the solution by attempting to gain access to main office resources from a desktop at the remote office. The test should also include using packet sniffers to monitor the network traffic at both offices and confirm that it is properly protected. If the test is unsuccessful, the administrators should troubleshoot the problem, make any necessary corrections or changes, then test the solution again.[120] Additional test actions should include implementing the restrictive packet filters and verifying them, and verifying that the correct algorithms are used. (For example, some IPsec implementations have a fallback policy that causes weaker algorithms to be used if the user-selected settings cannot be negotiated successfully; this could provide inadequate protection for communications.)

6.1.4 Analysis

Setting up an IPsec tunnel between Internet routers can be effective in connecting remote offices with multiple users to another network. It can reduce costs because remote offices need only Internet connectivity instead of a leased line. In addition, all traffic from the remote office could be routed though the main corporate firewall, which could decrease the costs and risks associated with administration of multiple firewalls. To set up this type of implementation, both routers would need to have a static IP address because the addresses would have to be entered into the IPsec configurations. In most cases, this is not an issue for the router at the main office, but it may be a problem for locations such as home offices that often use DSL or cable modem services, which may offer only dynamic IP addresses. Host-to-gateway solutions may be more practical for such situations.

In this case study, a gateway-to-gateway VPN was established between a remote office and the main office. An interesting variant on this scenario is a gateway-to-gateway VPN between the main office and the network of a business partner. In such a case, more stringent security measures may be needed to satisfy each organization's requirements for communication. Also, the organizations should establish a formal interconnection agreement that specifies the technical and security requirements for establishing, operating, and maintaining the interconnection, as well as documenting the terms and conditions for

---

118 The argument *xx.xx.xx.xx* should list the IP address of the other router's external interface, so the argument should be different on each router.

119 Appendix B.1 contains a sample configuration file from one of the routers.

120 The **debug crypto isakmp**, **debug crypto ipsec**, and **debug crypto engine** commands cause the router to display any errors related to the crypto implementation in the terminal window. This can be useful in determining why a connection is failing. Also, the **clear crypto sa** command can be used to clear part or all of the SA database, which may clear some errors.

sharing data and information resources in a secure manner. Appendix A contains more information on interconnection agreements.

In a gateway-to-gateway VPN between the organization and a business partner, each organization typically has control over its own VPN gateway. Accordingly, the organizations need to identify an acceptable out-of-band method for provisioning each other's gateways with the necessary authentication information, such as pre-shared keys or digital certificates. Another possible difference from the original scenario is that in the business partner scenario, both organizations should configure their packet filters to be as restrictive as possible from the beginning of the implementation. The organizations also need to coordinate their testing efforts and determine how a prototype for the solution can best be tested.

6.2 Protecting Wireless Communications

One of the system administrators for an organization often performs work from personal desktops and a personal laptop at home. The system administrator has a home office network that includes a host providing firewalling and NAT services, as well as wireless access for the desktops and laptop.[121] A recent security incident at the organization's main office involving improperly configured wireless access causes the system administrator to consider stronger security controls for the personal wireless network. The following sections describe how the system administrator evaluates options, identifies a viable solution, creates a design, and implements a prototype.

It is important to recognize that this solution does not protect communications between the system administrator's personal computers and the organization's networks and systems. The case study presented in Section 6.3 illustrates a solution for telecommuters and road warriors that provides protection for remote users. By implementing both solutions, the system administrator could have protection for work-related activity from the wireless clients to the organization's main network, as well as protection for personal and other activity on the wireless network.

6.2.1 Identifying Needs and Evaluating Options

As described below, the administrator considers a few options for protecting wireless communications:

- **Built-in 802.11b Security Features.** The administrator currently relies on the security features built in to 802.11b, such as Wired Equivalent Privacy (WEP) (which encrypts communications), for securing the wireless network. Unfortunately, these security features have numerous known security issues, including weaknesses in authentication and encryption. The administrator does not believe that these security features are sufficiently strong to defend the communications against increasing threats.[122]
- **Wi-Fi Protected Access (WPA) version 2.** WPA2 is a relatively new security specification that is intended to replace WEP and other weak security features.[123] Although it should provide a much more secure solution, the administrator's wireless access point is not WPA2-compliant.

---

[121] The administrator's equipment uses the 802.11b wireless standard. Although the newer 802.11g standard is becoming favored over 802.11b, from a network security perspective the standards are similar. Therefore, this case study would not be substantially different if 802.11g were in use instead of 802.11b.

[122] For more information on 802.11b security, see NIST SP 800-48, *Wireless Network Security: 802.11, Bluetooth and Handheld Devices*, available at http://csrc.nist.gov/publications/nistpubs/index html.

[123] The WPA2 security specification, which is closely related to the IEEE 802.11i protocol, supports AES-CCM and is intended to be FIPS 140-2 compliant. The original version of the security specification, known asWPA, is not FIPS 140-2 compliant. WPA uses the Temporal Key Integrity Protocol (TKIP) for confidentiality and integrity protection, while WPA2 uses the

- **Network Layer VPN.** The administrator could establish network layer VPNs over the wireless network that would protect the communications. The administrator's wireless access point cannot provide VPN services, so each VPN would need to go through the access point into a device that can support VPN services.[124] Each wireless device (e.g., desktop, laptop) needs to be configured as a VPN client, and a host (e.g., existing server, dedicated VPN device) needs to be set up to provide VPN services.
- **Data Link Layer VPN.** The administrator could purchase and deploy a data link layer VPN product, which is specifically designed to protect wireless communications. Such products typically involve installing VPN client software on each user's system and VPN server software. The server component needs to be incorporated into the access point. The administrator's existing access point is a low-end appliance, so VPN server software cannot be installed on it. Accordingly, to deploy a data link layer VPN, the administrator would need to establish a new access point, either by purchasing an appliance specifically designed to provide data link layer VPN services, or by adding access point capabilities to an existing server and then installing data link layer VPN server software on the server. In a larger environment, a data link layer VPN could provide an effective VPN solution at a reasonable cost, but in a small environment at relatively low risk, it is currently cost-prohibitive to deploy a data link layer VPN solution for wireless.

Although the network layer VPN solution requires the most setup and maintenance, it can provide adequate protection for communications and is compatible with the existing equipment. The administrator selects the network layer VPN solution and chooses a host-to-gateway architecture. This architecture allows communications to be secured between one or more wireless client hosts and a wired server providing VPN gateway services.

6.2.2 Designing the Solution

The system administrator considers possible network layer VPN solutions and selects IPsec. The client operating systems (Windows XP) have built-in IPsec clients, and the chosen VPN gateway's operating system (OpenBSD 3.5) also has built-in IPsec support. This should reduce the time needed to deploy the VPNs. Also, the administrator knows that IPsec can provide adequate protection for data confidentiality and integrity. Figure 6-2 illustrates the planned design for the VPN architecture. The IPsec tunnels protect the wireless communications between the clients (the laptop and desktops) and the access point. The tunnels also provide protection for communications on part of the wired network, although this protection is not needed. (Anyone that could gain unauthorized physical access to the wired network would also have access to the server, which could have much more severe consequences than network access.) NAT is performed by the cable router, which is outside the IPsec tunnel; accordingly, NAT and IPsec should not interfere with each other.

To clarify the architecture, consider how laptop A and desktop B could communicate with each other. Before any communications could occur, both hosts would need to establish wireless communications with the access point.[125] Since the IPsec protections are applied at the network layer, and wireless

---

Counter-Mode/CBC-MAC Protocol (CCMP). More information on WPA2, including key differences between WPA and WPA2, is available at http://wi-fi.org/OpenSection/protected_access.asp.

[124] Several wireless access point devices can provide VPN services, but such devices are typically designed for a large number of users. Small access points are unlikely to have VPN capabilities. Also, some access points that provide VPN services use IPsec only for the wired connection, and use WEP for the wireless connections.

[125] Because the laptop and the desktop are on the same subnet, by default each would attempt to establish connections directly to the other, without going through the IPsec gateway. This can most easily be addressed by reconfiguring routing on each host to send all traffic to the IPsec gateway. For example, the command **route add 192.168.0.27 mask 255.255.255.255**

communications occur at the data link layer, the connection can be established (and maintained) even though IPsec protections cannot yet be used. After the hosts have wireless communications in place, the hosts initiate IPsec tunnels to the VPN gateway. Once the tunnels are in place, laptop A can initiate a connection to desktop B through the IPsec tunnels. (The access point simply passes packets between tunnel endpoints, with no ability to see the contents of the packets.) When the VPN gateway receives laptop A's connection request, it decrypts and validates the packets, determines that they need to be sent to desktop B over its tunnel, applies IPsec protections to the packets, and sends them over the tunnel to desktop B.

After designing the architecture, the system administrator next considers other elements of the design and makes several decisions, including the following:

- **Authentication.** Because there are only a few hosts involved and they are located in a single house, a pre-shared key should provide adequate authentication with minimal effort (as compared to alternatives such as digital certificates).

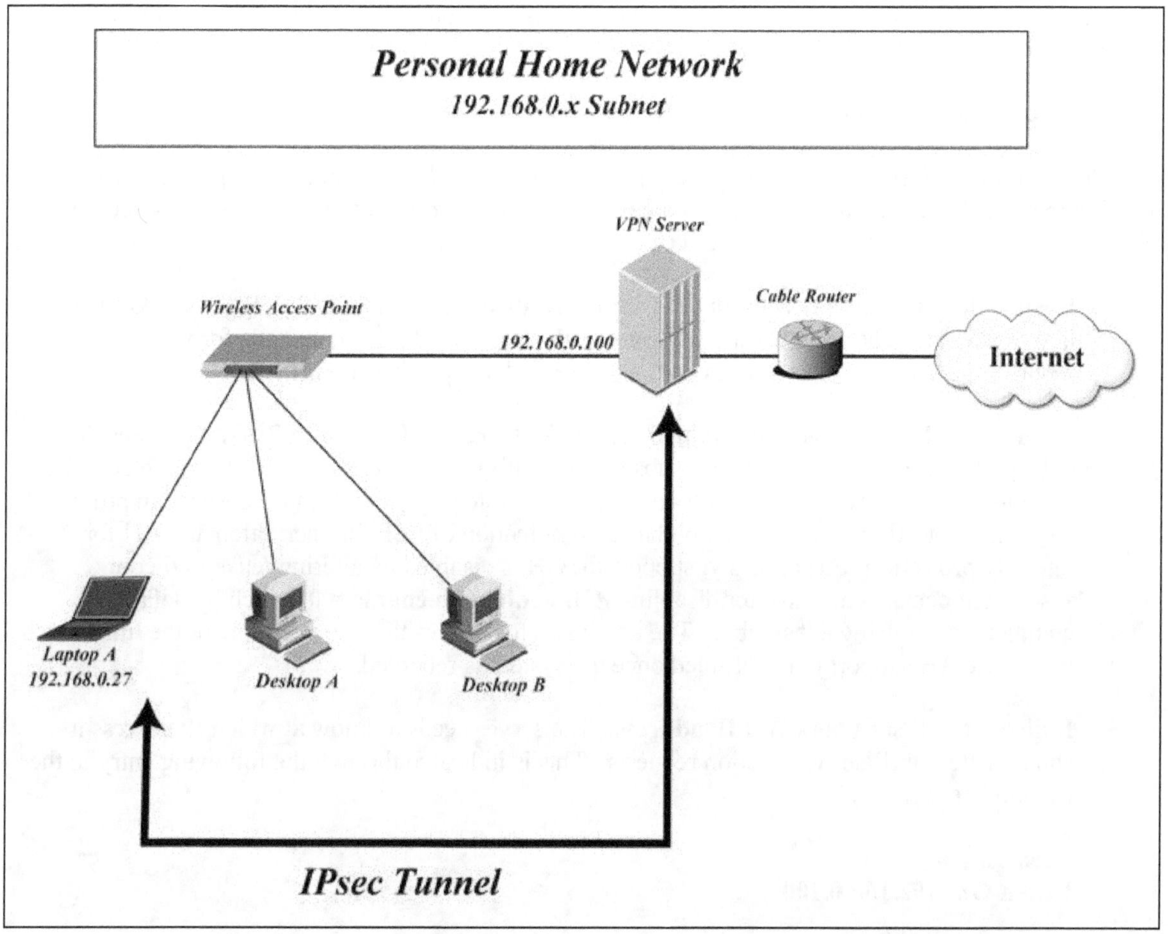

Figure 6-2. Host-to-Gateway VPN for Protecting Wireless Communications

---

192.168.0.100 would cause the Windows XP Home laptop to send its outgoing packets to the IPsec gateway even when it attempts to contact another host on the 192.168.0 subnet.

- **Encryption and Integrity Protection Algorithms.** The server supports several encryption algorithms, including Triple DES and AES, both of which provide adequately strong encryption for this situation. However, the desktop and laptop's built-in IPsec clients support Triple DES but not AES. Accordingly, Triple DES is chosen as the encryption algorithm. HMAC-SHA-1 is selected as the integrity protection algorithm because it provides adequate integrity protection and it is supported by both systems.

- **Packet Filters.** The administrator is not concerned about restricting traffic because the client and server systems are trusted. Because they use non-routable 192.168 network addresses, they cannot be directly contacted from Internet-based hosts. The cable router also has a set of filters that block incoming traffic. The server is also running a host-based firewall that restricts traffic on each of its network interfaces.[126]

6.2.3 Implementing a Prototype

The administrator performs the following steps to configure and test a prototype of the IPsec solution between the Windows XP Home laptop and the OpenBSD 3.5 server. Section 6.2.3.1 describes the configuration of the server, while Section 6.2.3.2 describes the laptop's configuration. The testing of the whole solution is detailed in Section 6.2.3.3.

6.2.3.1 Configuring the Server

The administrator performs the following steps to configure IPsec on the server. The process involves ensuring that the IPsec software is current and enabled, altering configuration files to specify settings, and rebooting the system so the settings take effect.

1. **Ensure that the current version of IPsec is installed.** In OpenBSD 3.5, IPsec support is built into the kernel. The administrator downloads the latest stable[127] source code for version 3.5 and rebuilds the kernel, which ensures that any IPsec-related patches are installed.

2. **Ensure that IPsec support is enabled.** By default, support for both ESP and AH is enabled. (The protocols cannot be used until subsequent configuration steps have been completed.) The administrator wishes to use ESP for encryption and integrity protection because it can provide adequate protection more efficiently than a combination of ESP for encryption and AH for integrity protection. Accordingly, support for AH is disabled by altering /etc/sysctl.conf. sysctl.conf contains an entry for disabling AH, **net.inet.ah.enable = 0**, which by default is commented out using a # symbol. The administrator deletes the # to uncomment the line, which will cause AH support to be disabled once the system is rebooted.

3. **Indicate the IPsec gateway's IP address.** The server needs to know at which IP address it should listen for IPsec connection requests. This is indicated through the following entry in the isakmpd.conf file:

   [General]
   Listen-On: 192.168.0.100

---

126 Although it is outside the scope of the case study to describe the firewall ruleset, the administrator needs to revise the ruleset to permit IPsec activity between the server and the clients.

127 The *stable* version of OpenBSD consists of the most recent major version release, plus necessary security and functionality-related updates.

4. **Define IDs for the endpoints.** In the isakmpd.conf file, the administrator defines two hosts, **Host-server** and **Host-laptop1**, and specifies their IP addresses. These IDs define labels that are referenced by other configuration entries within the isakmpd.conf file.

   [Host-server]
   ID-type = IPV4_ADDR
   Address = 192.168.0.100
   [Host-laptop1]
   ID-type = IPV4_ADDR
   Address = 192.168.0.27

5. **Specify the phase 1 configuration.**

   a. **Specify the phase 1 mode and cryptographic algorithms.** The administrator creates a section in the isakmpd.conf file that specifies the phase 1 settings, as follows:

      [Default-main-mode]
      DOI = IPSEC
      EXCHANGE_TYPE = ID_PROT[128]
      Transforms = 3DES-SHA

   b. **Specify the phase 1 endpoints, settings, and authentication.** The administrator creates a section in the isakmpd.conf that defines the phase 1 endpoints, specifies the authentication mechanism, and links to the phase 1 mode and cryptographic algorithm settings from the previous step. The configuration is as follows:

      [ISAKMP-peer-laptop1]
      Phase = 1
      Transport = udp[129]
      Local-address = 192.168.0.100
      Address = 192.168.0.27
      Configuration = Default-main-mode
      Authentication = +dEwaCIO+LiEkPELIbSiH24U8719mtDy0KG86NrtCkQ=[130]

   c. **Indicate which hosts may initiate phase 1 connections.** The administrator adds the following lines to isakmpd.conf to indicate which hosts may initiate phase 1 connections:

      [Phase 1]
      192.168.0.27 = ISAKMP-peer-laptop1

6. **Specify the phase 2 configuration.**

   a. **Specify the phase 2 protections.** The administrator creates a section in the isakmpd.conf file that specifies the phase 2 settings, as follows:

---

128 The ID_PROT parameter indicates that main mode should be used. Aggressive mode could be used by specifying AGGRESSIVE as the EXCHANGE_TYPE parameter.

129 By default, IKE uses UDP port 500.

130 This value was created by generating random values and then performing Base64 encoding on the values to convert them into printable characters. The following command can generate such a sequence on an OpenBSD 3.5 system by using the srandom random number generator and the OpenSSL command line tool:
/bin/dd if=/dev/srandom bs=1 count=32 | /usr/sbin/openssl base64

[Default-quick-mode]
DOI = IPSEC
EXCHANGE_TYPE = QUICK_MODE
Suites = QM-ESP-3DES-SHA-SUITE[131]

b. **Specify the phase 2 participants and settings.** The administrator creates a section in the isakmpd.conf that defines the phase 2 participants and links to the phase 2 settings from the previous step. The configuration is as follows:

[IPsec-laptop1-server]
Phase = 2
ISAKMP-peer = ISAKMP-peer-laptop1
Configuration = Default-quick-mode
Local-ID = server
Remote-ID = laptop1

c. **Indicate which hosts may initiate phase 2 connections.** The administrator adds the following lines to isakmpd.conf to indicate which hosts may initiate phase 2 connections:

[Phase 2]
Passive-connections = IPsec-laptop1-server

7. **Define the policy.** This policy only permits IPsec SAs to be established that meet certain mandatory requirements. The administrator updates the isakmpd.policy file as follows so that every IPsec SA must use ESP, 3DES for encryption, and HMAC-SHA for authentication:

Licensees: "passphrase: +dEwaCIO+LiEkPELIbSiH24U8719mtDy0KG86NrtCkQ="
Conditions: app_domain == "IPsec policy" &&
esp_present == "yes" &&
esp_enc_alg == "3des" &&
esp_auth_alg == "hmac-sha" -> "true";[132]

8. **Review the configuration.** After completing the configuration, the administrator reviews the server's configuration to ensure that all the necessary settings are in place.[133]

9. **Activate IPsec.** The administrator configures the system to activate IPsec by changing a parameter within the /etc/rc.conf.local file.[134] The default setting, **isakmpd_flags = NO**, indicates that isakmpd is disabled. Changing the setting to **isakmpd_flags = ""** will cause isakmpd to be activated when the configuration file is next used. The administrator reboots the system, which causes the changes made to all the configuration files to take effect.

10. **Confirm that IKE is running.** The administrator confirms that IKE is running through commands such as the following:

---

[131] This suite does not explicitly specify tunnel or transport mode, nor does it list a Diffie-Hellman group. By default, suites use tunnel mode and Diffie-Hellman group 2.

[132] The administrator can specify many other conditions here, such as whether perfect forward secrecy is being used, which Diffie-Hellman group is used, and whether tunnel or transport mode is requested. This allows the server to deny access to clients that do not use the expected settings.

[133] Appendix B.2 contains sample isakmpd.conf and isakmpd.policy files that correspond to the previous steps.

[134] By default, the /etc/rc.conf file is the primary source of service configuration information, and it has isakmpd disabled by default. Many administrators create a separate /etc/rc.conf.local file, which overrides the default settings in /etc/rc.conf. If isakmpd is enabled in /etc/rc.conf.local, the isakmpd setting in /etc/rc.conf is ignored.

- **ps –ax | grep isakmpd**, which should indicate that the isakmpd process is running
- **netstat –an | grep 500**, which should show that IKE is listening on UDP port 500 of the desired network interface.[135]

6.2.3.2 Configuring the Laptop

After completing the server configuration, the administrator next configures the laptop to be an IPsec client. The steps performed to achieve this are as follows:

1. **Ensure that the laptop has a current IPsec client.** Because Windows XP has a built-in IPsec client, the administrator runs Microsoft Update and confirms that the laptop already has all service packs and hotfixes applied, which means that the IPsec client is up-to-date.

2. **Load the IPsec configuration utility.** To define an IPsec configuration for the client, the administrator needs to use the built-in IPsec configuration utility. To run it, the administrator loads the Microsoft Management Console by executing **mmc.exe**. The administrator then accesses the **File** menu, selects **Add/Remove Snap-in**, and adds the **IP Security Policy Management** snap-in.

3. **Create a new IPsec configuration entry.** The administrator right-clicks on **IP Security Policies in Local Computer** and selects **IP Security Policy.**[136] This launches the IP Security Policy Wizard. The administrator provides a name for the IPsec configuration—in this case, **Wireless Protection.**

4. **Configure authentication.** The IP Security Policy Wizard prompts the administrator to specify an authentication method. In this case, the administrator configures the client to use a preshared key and specifies the key **+dEwaCIO+LiEkPELIbSiH24U8719mtDy0KG86NrtCkQ=** (which is displayed in plaintext). The wizard ends; the administrator then edits the IP Security Policy to specify other IPsec settings, as described in the following steps.

5. **Create first IP security rule.** The administrator needs to define two IP security rules—one for the communications from the laptop to the server, and one for the communications from the server to the laptop. The administrator first creates a rule for laptop to server communications, as follows:

   a. **Define the packet filter.** Because the administrator does not wish to perform fine-grained filtering, he specifies the packet filter as permitting all protocols and ports from the laptop (**<My IP Address>**) to any destination (**<Any IP Address>**). This is done from the **IP Filter List** tab.

   b. **Specify the cryptography algorithms and SA lifetimes.** From the **Filter Action** tab, the administrator configures the client to require protection for all communications through the **Require Security** option. The client is then set to **Negotiate Security**, with ESP selected to provide encryption using 3DES and integrity protection using SHA1. The client is also configured to generate a new key every 900 seconds or 100000 kilobytes.

   c. **Specify the ESP mode.** On the **Tunnel Setting** tab, the administrator enters the IP address of the server, 192.168.0.100.

---

[135] The administrator could display all listening ports by issuing the following command: **netstat –an | grep LIST**.

[136] *IP Security Policy* is the Windows XP term for an IPsec configuration.

6. **Create second IP security rule.** The administrator creates a rule for server to laptop communications, as follows:

    a. **Define the packet filter.** Because the administrator does not wish to perform fine-grained filtering, he specifies the packet filter as permitting all protocols and ports from any source (**<Any IP Address>**) to the laptop (**<My IP Address>**).

    b. **Specify the cryptography algorithms and SA lifetimes.** The administrator configures the cryptography algorithms and SA lifetimes identically to the first security rule's settings.

    c. **Specify the ESP mode.** The administrator specifies tunnel mode by entering the IP address of the laptop, 192.168.0.27.

7. **Review the configuration.** After completing the configuration, the administrator reviews the client's configuration to ensure that all the necessary settings are in place.

8. **Enable the client.** From the MMC screen, the administrator right-clicks on the **Wireless Protection** configuration and selects **Assign**, which activates the configuration.

6.2.3.3 Testing the Solution

After completing the laptop configuration, the administrator tests the solution to ensure that the laptop and server are establishing and maintaining connections properly. The administrator uses the laptop to access various resources on the internal network and on external networks (e.g., public Web servers) and monitors the traffic using a packet sniffer on the laptop to confirm that the traffic is properly protected. The packet sniffer can also be very helpful when troubleshooting issues because it can indicate where connections are failing, such as a phase 1 request from the laptop generating no response from the server. Windows XP also offers built-in tools such as the IP Security Monitor that can be helpful with troubleshooting IPsec client issues.[137]

6.2.4 Analysis

Establishing IPsec tunnels to protect wireless communications can be effective in protecting the communications from eavesdroppers. Using the IPsec software provided with the endpoints instead of acquiring additional hardware or software meant that there were no financial costs for the administrator, and that deployment time was reduced. Because the administrator has complete control over the environment and the network architecture is very simple, this deployment was very easy. Still, this model could be used in more complex deployments to protect wireless communications, such as enterprise networks. Additional considerations for such deployments include the need for stronger physical security controls on the endpoints, and the identification or creation of an appropriate system to house the IPsec gateway.

6.3 Protecting Communications for Remote Users

For a few years, an agency has been conducting a research study that includes participation from a small number of external consultants from both public and private organizations throughout the United States. As part of the study, the participating consultants collect data and transfer it to the agency frequently via File Transfer Protocol (FTP). (Because some of the data files are more than a gigabyte in size, they are

[137] For more information on troubleshooting capabilities provided by Windows XP, see Microsoft's documentation located at http://www.microsoft.com/resources/documentation/windows/xp/all/proddocs/en-us/sag_ipsec_tools.mspx.

far too large to be transferred via e-mail.) The agency also generates daily reports that incorporate recently received data transfers; the external consultants can download these reports from the FTP server as needed, as well as other reports, documentation, and other materials related to the research study. As a result of recent legislation regarding privacy, the agency has determined that the confidentiality of the data being transferred needs to be protected in transit so that unauthorized parties cannot access it. The agency is seeking a solution that will provide adequate protection for the data at minimal cost, and with minimal changes to the agency's IT infrastructure. The following sections describe how the agency evaluates options, identifies a viable solution, creates a design, and implements a prototype.

6.3.1 Identifying Needs and Evaluating Options

As described below, the agency considers a few options for protecting the data transfers between the external organizations and the existing FTP server:

- **Network Layer Solution: Network Layer VPN.** The organization could establish network layer VPNs between the external organizations and the agency's main office. The VPN tunnels would provide access to the FTP resources and protect the data being transferred. The organization considers each possible network layer VPN architecture, as follows:

  - A gateway-to-gateway VPN solution is cost-prohibitive because of the number of external sites using the solution and because each external organization would need a compatible VPN gateway.

  - The agency already has a host-to-gateway VPN implementation. A VPN gateway at the main office supports secure communications between telecommuting employees' computers and the main office. A host-to-gateway solution would allow the organization to use its existing VPN gateway, eliminating additional hardware costs. Each host would need VPN client software installed, but this would be done by the participating organizations, so additional labor would be limited to supporting the organizations in performing the installations and troubleshooting issues. The organization would need to pay for additional VPN client licenses.

  - Another option is the use of host-to-host VPNs. This option requires identifying and implementing a new technology, which involves substantially more cost than leveraging the current host-to-gateway implementation.

- **Transport Layer Solution: Web-Based FTP Solution.** The organization could provide Web-based access to FTP resources. This could be accomplished by deploying a secured Web-based FTP server at the main office and allowing the external organizations to access this server over the Internet through Web browsers. The communications would use the TLS protocol over HTTP to protect the confidentiality and integrity of data. Although this solution would meet the requirement to protect the data in transit, it would require the organization to deploy, secure, and maintain a Web server. Another potential issue with the solution is that by default, users would not be authenticated before establishing a TCP connection to the FTP server. Since FTP authentication is based on a username and password, using a stronger authentication mechanism in addition to the standard FTP authentication would provide better security.

- **Application Layer Solution: File Encryption.** Instead of encrypting communications, an application layer solution could encrypt the files themselves, which could then be transferred through non-encrypted communications. Using a public key from the agency, the external organizations could encrypt their data files and then FTP the files to the server over public networks. The data files on the server could be decrypted by the organization as needed.

Although file encryption is a reasonable solution for transferring files to the agency's server, it is not well-suited for protecting reports and other files that may be downloaded from the server by the external organizations. Such files would need to be encrypted so that the external organizations could decrypt them. As organizations join or leave the agency's study, or other changes occur to the set of valid keys, all files would need to be encrypted using the new set of keys. The agency could establish a shared key for all external organizations, but this would increase the risk of unauthorized access, reduce accountability, and still require considerable maintenance effort, such as distributing new keys in an out-of-band manner.

After further investigations into security, ease of deployment, and cost, the organization selects the network layer VPN solution and chooses to use its existing host-to-gateway architecture. Since the components of the solution have already been implemented and tested, only a few steps are needed to modify the existing solution so it provides adequate protection for the external organizations' FTP usage. It is important to note that this solution protects FTP traffic only between the external organizations' hosts and the main office's VPN gateway; the traffic between the VPN gateway and the FTP server is not protected.

6.3.2 Designing the Solution

The solution is based on the agency's existing Lucent IPsec gateway. The agency has previously purchased 200 licenses for the Lucent IPsec client, about 50 of which are unused currently. The Lucent IPsec client software is compatible with several versions of Microsoft Windows, including those run by the external users of the FTP server. The solution for protecting FTP should be able to use the Lucent client, which should reduce the time needed to deploy the VPNs. The VPN gateway is lightly utilized, so an additional VPN gateway is not needed for the external organizations' FTP usage.

Figure 6-3 illustrates the planned design for the VPN architecture. The external organizations and the main office are on different networks that can reach each other through the Internet. The strategy is to establish an IPsec tunnel between an external system and the main office VPN gateway. Data sent between the external system and the VPN gateway will be encrypted, while data between the VPN gateway and the FTP server will not be encrypted. The tunnel will stay intact until the external system or the VPN gateway manually terminates the tunnel or the connection is inactive for a certain period of time. The gateway and client software support UDP encapsulation, so telecommuting clients that are on NAT networks can enable UDP encapsulation in the IPsec client and use the IPsec solution.

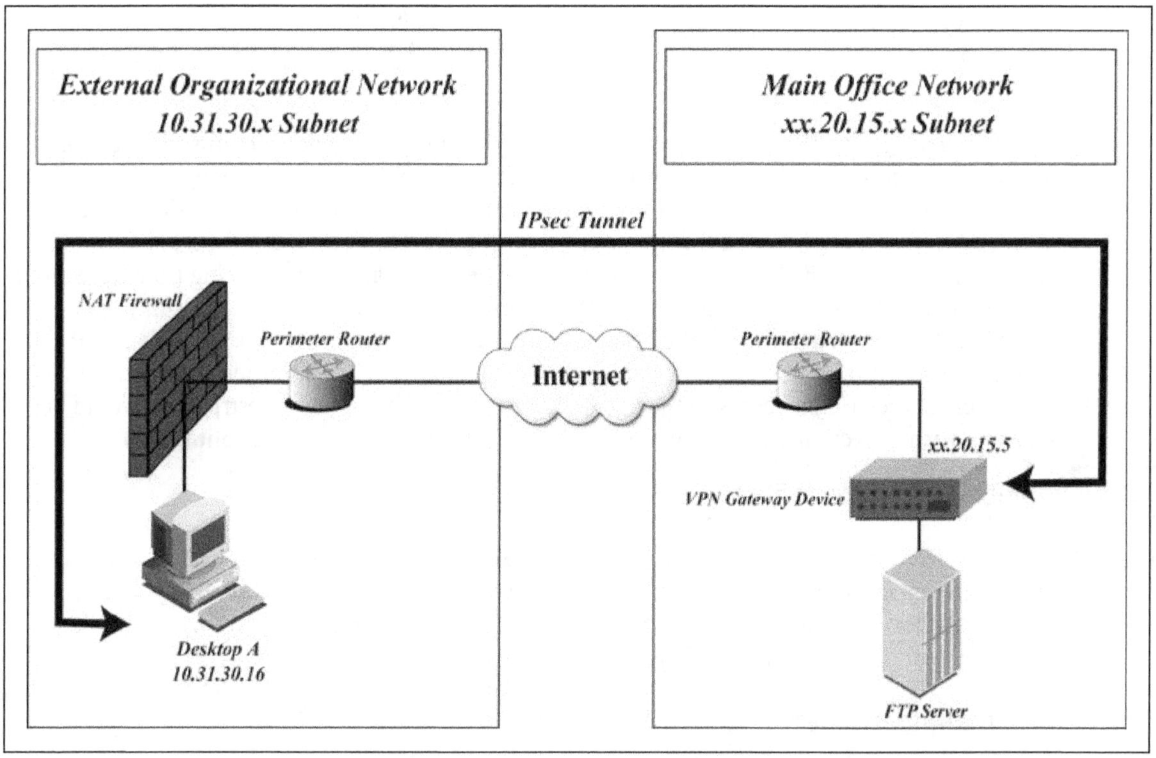

Figure 6-3. Host-to-Gateway VPN for Protecting Communications

After designing the architecture, the organization next considers other elements of the design and makes several decisions, including the following:

- **Authentication.** For initial testing of the solution, a pre-shared key can be used in combination with username and password authentication to authenticate the external test user. In the actual deployment of the solution, users will be authenticated through digital certificates issued by the agency's certification authority. The digital certificates will be sent to the external organizations through an out-of-band method; each organization will then need to place a copy of the digital certificate onto each IPsec client machine, and the IPsec client will be configured to use the digital certificate. When a tunnel needs to be established, the client will send the certificate to the VPN gateway for authentication.
- **Encryption and Integrity Protection Algorithms.** The VPN gateway supports multiple encryption algorithms, including Triple DES and DES, but not AES. Triple DES is the strongest encryption algorithm supported by both the gateway and the client software, so it is chosen as the encryption algorithm. HMAC-SHA-1 is selected as the integrity protection algorithm because it provides adequate integrity protection and it is supported by both systems.
- **Packet Filters.** To restrict the external organizations' usage as much as possible, the IPsec packet filters should be configured to permit only FTP traffic over the VPN tunnel. Unlike most protocols, FTP is a multi-session protocol; it maintains a TCP connection for an FTP control channel, and establishes a separate TCP connection for each FTP data transfer requested over the control channel. The gateway supports passive mode FTP, in which the client system initiates all

FTP data connections.[138] Accordingly, the packet filters should be configured to permit only FTP control channels and passive mode FTP data connections initiated by the external clients to the FTP server.

- **Split Tunneling.** The IPsec client offers multiple split tunneling-related settings; by default, it allows split tunneling but blocks all unsolicited traffic sent to the client. Although completely forbidding split tunneling could provide slightly stronger security, the default setting is more balanced between security and functionality. If the client is configured to prevent split tunneling, users cannot use any other network resources while the large data files are being transferred to the FTP server, which could take hours. Also, the packet filters tightly restrict access into the agency's network through the VPN gateway, so even if a remote attacker took over an FTP client's system, little access could be gained through split tunneling. (For telecommuters that have much less restricted access to the agency's network, split tunneling restrictions would be more important. Section 4.2.1.2 contains additional information regarding split tunneling.)

6.3.3 Implementing a Prototype

The VPN gateway administrator performs the following steps to configure and test a prototype of the IPsec solution between an external test system and the Lucent VPN gateway. Section 6.3.3.1 describes the configuration of the VPN gateway device, while Section 6.3.3.2 describes the external system's configuration. The testing of the whole solution is detailed in Section 6.3.3.3.

6.3.3.1 Configuring the Server

The administrator performs the following steps to configure the Lucent VPN gateway to provide protection for the FTP server usage. These settings are specified in the Lucent Security Management VPN administration server GUI. Because the VPN gateway is an existing solution, the following instructions assume that it has been maintained properly (e.g., fully patched, properly secured).

1. **Create a separate user account for each IPsec user.** Account generation is needed to identify the specific users as well as set authentication parameters for those users. For initial testing, the administrator creates a temporary test account by right-clicking in the **Users** submenu and selecting **New User**. The administrator configures the user account with the following parameters:

   User ID: TestUser
   Authentication Service: Local Password
   Password: j9%L$s4F
   Verify Password: j9%L$s4F
   Allowed Source IP Address: *[139]

2. **Associate user accounts to user groups.** To reduce administration, user accounts are added to specific groups; VPN rules are then created for each group rather than for individual users. The administrator creates a temporary test group by going to the **User Groups** submenu, right-

---

138 The alternative to passive mode FTP is active mode, in which the server initiates each FTP data connection to the client. From a network security perspective, it is often preferable to have the client initiate all connections to the server, because this can be specified clearly in packet filters. From a functional perspective, active mode data connections often will not work when NAT is in use because the client supplies its real IP address to the server when it requests the data connection. The server then tries to initiate the connection to the client's real IP address instead of the NATted IP address. Because of such problems, many organizations only permit passive mode FTP through their network perimeters.

139 The * indicates that any source IP address is acceptable. Although it does provide stronger security to list a specific IP address for this field, it is not feasible to do so for telecommuters and others that use dynamic IP addresses.

clicking and selecting **New User Group**, then entering a name for the group—in this case, **TestUserGroup**. The administrator then selects the **TestUser** account created in Step 1 and associates the user with the group by clicking the **Add** button.

3. **Set the tunnel parameters.** The gateway needs to know what parameters to use when establishing tunnels for the FTP client systems. The VPN gateway administrator sets the parameters for the device, tunnel endpoint, hosts behind the tunnel and group key. In addition, the administrator configures both the ISAKMP Proposal, which sets up the tunnel, and the IPsec Proposal, which sets up the encryption, by right clicking and selecting **New Client to LAN tunnel** in the Client to LAN submenu.

   a. **Specify which resources the users can access.** On the main tab, the administrator enters the following settings:

      Device: TestUserGroup
      Tunnel Endpoint: xx.20.15.5
      Hosts Behind Tunnel: FTP_Server

   b. **Set the pre-shared key for testing.** On the Parameters tab, the administrator enters the following setting:

      Group Key: FhwkpoaYhsDDkamWutwH[140]

   c. **Specify the phase 1 settings.** The administrator right-clicks and selects **New Client to LAN tunnel**, then enters the following settings for the **ISAKMP Proposal**:

      D-H Group: Group 2
      Encryption Type: Triple DES
      Authentication Type: HMAC SHA1

   d. **Specify the phase 2 settings.** The administrator enters the following settings for the **IPsec Proposal**:

      Protocol: ESP-50
      Encryption Type: Triple DES
      Authentication Type: HMAC SHA1
      SA Lifetime: 144000 (4 hours)[141]

4. **Create a ruleset to allow FTP traffic between the gateway and the FTP server.** The VPN gateway administrator creates a ruleset allowing only FTP traffic to pass through the gateway to the server. The VPN gateway administrator creates the ruleset by right clicking and selecting **New Brickzone Ruleset** in the Brickzone rulesets submenu. The administrator then performs the following steps:

   a. **Specify the ruleset.** The administrator enters the following settings:

      Name: External System Access to Main Office
      Direction: Into Zone
      Source: TestUserGroup
      Destination: FTP_Server

---

140 The group key needs to be at least 20 characters long and is generated by the administrator.

141 The default lifetime is 4 hours. The lifetime can be set between 2 minutes and 48 hours.

Service: FTP
Action: VPN

b. **Permit two-way traffic.** The administrator selects the **Authorize Return Channel** option from the Advanced tab. This option allows bi-directional traffic to be permitted within a single rule. Because the gateway is session-oriented, this feature allows packets to come back from an established session.

5. **Assign the new ruleset to the "inside" VPN interface.** The VPN gateway administrator assigns the newly created ruleset to the "inside" VPN by clicking on the **Main Office Brick** in the Bricks submenu and entering the following parameters:

   Zone Ruleset: External System Access to Main Office
   Port: Ether 1[142]
   Tunnel Endpoint: xx.20.15.5
   Hosts Behind Tunnel: FTP_Server

6.3.3.2 Configuring the System

After completing the VPN gateway configuration, the administrator configures an externally located test system to be an IPsec client. The steps performed to achieve this are as follows:

1. **Load the latest Lucent IPsec client onto the system.** The administrator double clicks on the ipsec-6.0.1.exe executable file located on the IPsec client software CD provided by Lucent, and follows the corresponding steps to perform the client installation.

2. **Configure the IPsec client.** To configure the client, the administrator first runs the client by choosing the **Lucent IPsec Client** icon from the Start menu. Once the client has started, the administrator configures the tunnel settings by clicking on **Secure Connection**. The administrator then sets the following parameters:

   Tunnel Name: External System Access to Main Office
   Primary Tunnel End Point: xx.20.15.5
   User Identity: TestUser
   Password: j9%L$s4F
   Group Key: FhwkpoaYhsDDkamWutwH

3. **Test the tunnel settings.** Once the parameters have been entered, the administrator clicks the **Enable** button. Upon tunnel creation, the following message appears:

   Enable Secure Connection successful.
   Session will end at: Aug 28, 10:25 AM
   IP Address for local presence is: 10.31.30.16

6.3.3.3 Testing the Solution

After completing the configuration of the VPN gateway and the external test system, the VPN gateway administrator tests the solution to ensure that the external system can successfully establish a secure tunnel between the VPN gateway and transfer encrypted FTP traffic through the tunnel. The

---

[142] This setting indicates which port the interface is on. In this particular device, the ports range from 0 to 3, and the inside interface is on port 1.

administrator runs the IPsec client, which successfully establishes a secure tunnel through the IPsec client. The administrator then connects to the FTP server through the tunnel, authenticates using an FTP username and password, and uploads and downloads test files of various sizes. (This should include using the FTP client both in active and passive mode to confirm that only passive mode works.) Tests should also ascertain that the VPN gateway will only negotiate IPsec tunnels for the approved algorithm (in this case, Triple DES); will only allow FTP traffic that is encrypted with the approved algorithm; and will block traffic that is not encrypted or that is encrypted with any other algorithm (e.g. DES).[143] The administrator also attempts to connect to the FTP server using application protocols other than FTP, and to connect to other hosts on the agency's network (using FTP and other protocols), to confirm that the VPN gateway permits FTP usage only with the FTP server and only for the test user. The administrator monitors the VPN gateway's logs for errors that indicate problems with the connection. The gateway's log report generation tool can be useful when troubleshooting issues because it can indicate where connections are failing, or where traffic is being dropped. The administrator also deploys a packet sniffer on the external test network to confirm that the traffic is being protected.

6.3.4 Analysis

IPsec tunnels established from external systems to a trusted gateway can be effective for protecting sensitive information from eavesdroppers. Using the existing IPsec client software and IPsec gateway eliminated the need to purchase additional hardware or software and greatly reduced design and implementation time. The only significant changes to the existing configuration were to create user accounts for the external organizations and to specify a policy for their FTP server use. This implementation was very simple because the agency had already implemented a solution for telecommuter access. For the FTP server need, the existing telecommuter solution was modified to provide very restricted access to the organization's network for the FTP users. Noteworthy elements of the existing telecommuter solution, compared to the FTP-only solution, are as follows:

- **Available Resources.** The telecommuters can access more of the agency's computing resources than the FTP-only users. The agency has identified all hosts that the telecommuters need to access and determined which protocols need to be used for each host. For example, telecommuters can access several web servers through HTTP and HTTPS, the corporate directory server through LDAP, and the corporate antivirus server through FTP (to download software and signature updates). The telecommuters' group on the IPsec gateway and the packet filters are configured to permit access to the required hosts only.

- **Split Tunneling.** Because the telecommuters can communicate with dozens of the agency's hosts using a variety of protocols, and each telecommuter's system is connected the telecommuters present substantially more risk to the agency. Therefore, split tunneling is not permitted so that the potential impact to the agency from telecommuter systems compromised by malware and other means is limited.

- **Client Host Security.** In addition to forbidding split tunneling, the agency has established other policies regarding telecommuter use of IPsec. Specifically, telecommuters are required to have up-to-date antivirus and antispyware software installed and enabled on their systems, as well as a personal firewall that monitors incoming and outgoing network traffic. The primary purpose of these policies is to prevent client hosts from becoming compromised and limit the potential impact of any compromises that occur.

---

[143] Some implementations will allow negotiations to silently fall back to a default algorithm (commonly DES), even when configured for a stronger algorithm. Testing is necessary to ensure that this does not happen.

7. Future Directions

This section briefly discusses some of the future directions of IPsec. At this time, the IETF is finalizing a set of revised IPsec standards, as well as several extensions to IPsec. This section provides a brief discussion of the new standards and pointers to additional information. The next part of this section examines issues related to extending IPsec to handle multicast traffic. The final topic addressed in this section is IPv6. Some background and general information on IPv6 is provided, along with a brief discussion on the effect that IPv6 deployments are expected to have on IPsec.

7.1 Revised IPsec Standards

The IP Security Protocol Working Group of the IETF has developed dozens of RFCs and Internet-Drafts related to updating IPsec standards.[144] As discussed in Section 3.3.5, one of the proposed standards is for IKEv2; it makes significant changes to the performance and capabilities of IKE. There are also proposed standards for version 3 of ESP, AH, and the general IPsec architecture and processing model; however, the changes for these are not as major as the changes in IKE. There is also a proposed standard for performing UDP encapsulation of IP packets, which is mentioned in Section 4.2.1.1. This is a technique to overcome issues involving NAT. Once vendors begin to add support for these features into their products, this should lead to improved IPsec implementations.

7.2 Support for Multicast Traffic

Multicast traffic refers to sending a packet to an IP address that is designated as a multicast address; one or more hosts that are specifically interested in the communication then receive copies of that single packet. This differs from *broadcast traffic*, which causes packets to be distributed to all hosts on a subnet, because multicast traffic will only be sent to hosts that are interested in it. Multicasting is most often used to stream audio and video. For the sender, there are two primary advantages of using multicast. First, the sender only needs to create and send one packet, instead of creating and sending a different packet to each recipient. Second, the sender does not need to keep track of who the actual recipients are. Multicasting can also be advantageous from a network perspective, because it reduces network bandwidth usage.

The current version of IPsec cannot provide protection for multicast traffic, because IPsec was designed specifically for protecting communications between two specific points, not among many points at once. Each multicast packet may have many recipients, which raises many IPsec-related issues. For example, a thousand hosts may all need to decrypt the same packet, but sharing the secret key among them is not a sound security practice.[145] Another issue is that many different hosts may be sending packets to the multicast address. Again, each of these hosts needs to share the same authentication mechanism. This means that one source host can spoof the identity of another source host, and that the recipients may not be able to detect it, eliminating IPsec's source authentication capability. Also, the antireplay protection provided by the sequence number is not available because multiple senders could simultaneously generate legitimate packets that happen to use the same sequence number. These are but a few examples of the problems caused by attempting to have IPsec provide support for multicast traffic.

Researchers have been attempting for several years to find a viable way to extend IPsec so it can support multicast traffic without losing its methods of protection, particularly source authentication. One of the

---

[144] A current list of the working group's RFCs and Internet-Drafts is available at http://www.ietf.org/html.charters/OLD/ipsec-charter.html.

[145] If the hosts share the same secret key, and one host should no longer have access to the multicast traffic, then the secret key needs to be updated on all the hosts in a timely manner. Distributing the new key in a secure manner to all the hosts may be extremely challenging.

biggest challenges is to find a solution that is not too resource-intensive. Because multicast is typically used for applications such as streaming video that are constantly generating packets, IPsec cannot add too much overhead to the processing of each packet or the applications' functionality may be seriously impaired. Researchers expect that multiple multicast solutions may be created, each addressing a particular multicast need (e.g., single sender multicast, multicast groups with a small number of members). It is outside the scope of this document to examine the proposed methods. Detailed information is available from research efforts that have been seeking solutions for multicast security issues, including the Group Security (GSEC) Research Group within the Internet Research Task Force (IRTF)[146] and the Multicast Security (MSEC) Working Group within the IETF.[147]

7.3 Interoperability with PKI

During the development of IPsec standards, the IETF IPsec working group discussed but did not have time to finalize standards related to PKI. There is an increasing need to set a standard for PKI and IPsec interoperability so that IPsec services can use digital certificates. Few IPsec implementations have used certificates, in large part due to the lack of standards. Consequently, a new IETF working group, Profiling Use of PKI in IPsec (PKI4IPSEC), is currently discussing this topic and beginning to develop proposed standards.[148] The group plans on developing specific documentation for how IKE should handle certificates, as well as a standard for certificate management in the context of IPsec implementations.

7.4 IKE Mobility and Multihoming

The IETF's IKEv2 Mobility and Multihoming (MOBIKE) working group[149] is currently developing extensions to IKEv2. The extensions will allow IKE to function more smoothly in cases of IPsec host mobility (the host's actual IP address changes)[150]. For example, a host could change IP addresses after establishing a session and not need to reauthenticate or rekey to sustain communications. The extensions will also improve the support for multihoming (a single host has multiple IP addresses). Protocols such as the Stream Control Transmission Protocol (SCTP)[151] currently incur substantial overhead when being used with IPsec.

7.5 IPv6

The previous sections of this guide addressed IPsec as it is implemented for IP version 4 (IPv4), which is the version of IP in use on nearly all networks. Many years ago, to address various shortcomings with IPv4 (including the lack of various security features and the limited number of available addresses), standards were developed for a new version of IP called IPv6.[152] IPv6 provides a much larger address space that is expected to meet the addressing needs for all networked devices for the foreseeable future.

---

146 The IRTF home page is located at http://www.irtf.org/. For more information on the GSEC Research Group, visit their Web page at http://www.securemulticast.org/gsec-index.htm.

147 The IETF home page is located at http://www.ietf.org/. For more information on the MSEC Working Group, visit their Web page at http://www.securemulticast.org/msec-index.htm.

148 For more information on the PKI4IPSEC Working Group, visit their Web page at http://www.ietf.org/html.charters/pki4ipsec-charter.html.

149 For more information on the MOBIKE Working Group, visit their IETF Web page at http://www.ietf.org/html.charters/mobike-charter.html or their additional Web page at http://www.vpnc.org/ietf-mobike/.

150 This should not be confused with a network device performing NAT, which changes the host's apparent address to outside parties. Mobility refers to the actual IP address of the host itself being changed.

151 More information on SCTP is available in RFC 3286, *An Introduction to the Stream Control Transmission Protocol (SCTP)*, available at http://www.ietf.org/rfc/rfc3286.txt, and RFC 2960, *Stream Control Transmission Protocol*, available at http://www.ietf.org/rfc/rfc2960.txt.

152 More information on IPv6 is available from the IP Version 6 Working Group of the IETF at http://www.ietf.org/html.charters/ipv6-charter.html.

The RFCs for IPv6 mandate the inclusion of IPsec to preserve the confidentiality and integrity of network communications.[153]

When IPv6 was developed, the intention was that it would provide end-to-end security for all network communications, eliminating the need for intermediate security layers such as firewalls. Hosts would simply be able to establish tunnels to other hosts without prior preparatory measures. However, because of increased threats and security needs, most organizations are unlikely to rely only on the IPsec services implemented on individual hosts to provide sufficient protection for all network communications. The common models that evolve for providing network security in IPv6 environments are likely to be similar to those currently used for IPv4 networks.

Although the IPv6 standard has been in place for some time, the adoption of IPv6 has occurred much more slowly than originally expected; to date, it has been implemented in only a limited capacity in the United States. It has taken considerable time for software vendors to add IPv6 support to operating systems and applications. Network infrastructures have to become IPv6-compatible, which often means replacing existing equipment. The implementation of IPv6 has been increasing recently, and it appears that over the next several years, it may become widespread. Legacy implementations of IPsec on IPv4 networks are likely to continue to be used for some time after that, perhaps indefinitely. It is expected that IPsec will be used in IPv4 and IPv6 environments for many years to come.

---

[153] Although the IPv6 standards include IPsec, vendors implementing IPv6 are under no obligation to include IPsec, although it is expected that most will.

Appendix A—Policy Considerations

As mentioned in Section 4, organizations should develop IPsec-related policy and use it as the foundation for their IPsec planning and implementation activities. This appendix presents examples of common IPsec-related policy considerations that address the confidentiality, integrity, and availability of the IPsec implementation, as well as the conditions constituting its acceptable use. The appendix focuses on policy considerations for three sample scenarios: a gateway-to-gateway VPN between two offices of a single organization, a gateway-to-gateway VPN between two business partners, and a host-to-gateway VPN for telecommuting employees of an organization.

The examples provided in this appendix are intended only to provide a starting point for developing IPsec-related policy. Each organization needs to develop its own policy based on its environment, requirements, and needs. Also, many of the policy considerations in this section might already be addressed through an organization's existing policies. The examples in this appendix are not comprehensive; organizations should identify additional IPsec-related considerations that apply to their environments.

A.1 Communications with a Remote Office Network

In this scenario, an organization wants to establish an IPsec VPN to protect communications between its main office's network and a remote office's network. This VPN would be created by having the organization deploy and manage an IPsec gateway on each network, and configuring the gateways so that they protect communications between the networks through an IPsec tunnel as needed. This scenario assumes that the same policies apply to the main office and remote office networks. The policy consideration examples listed in this section are divided into two groups: items specific to the IPsec gateway devices and management servers, and items specific to the hosts and people using the IPsec tunnel.

A.1.1 IPsec Gateway Devices and Management Servers

Items that are typically part of VPN policy for gateway devices and management servers include the following:

- Roles and responsibilities related to IPsec gateway operations
- Definition for where VPNs tunnels should terminate (e.g., between the border router and firewall, on the firewall)
- Security controls that are required to monitor the unencrypted network traffic, such as network-based intrusion detection systems or antivirus software, and their acceptable placement in the network architecture relative to the IPsec gateways
- Authentication requirements for IPsec gateway administrators (e.g., two-factor authentication). This could also include requirements to change all default manufacturer passwords on the gateways and management servers, to have a separate account for each administrator, to change administrator passwords on a regular basis, and to disable or delete an administrator account as soon as it is no longer needed.
- Authentication requirements for IPsec tunnel users, if any. This should include a requirement for how often user accounts are audited.
- Authentication requirements for the IPsec gateway devices

- Security requirements for the IPsec gateway devices and IPsec management servers. For example, an organization might require a firewall to be deployed between an IPsec gateway device and its users, and configured to block all traffic not explicitly approved for use with the IPsec implementation. An organization might also require certain security controls on the IPsec gateway devices and management servers, such as host-based firewalls and antivirus software.
- What information should be kept in audit logs, how long it should be maintained, and how often it should be reviewed
- Requirements for remediating vulnerabilities in the IPsec gateway devices and management servers
- Which types of traffic should be protected by IPsec tunnels, and what types of protection should be applied to each type of traffic
- What types of protection should be applied to communications between an IPsec gateway and an IPsec management server.

A.1.2 Hosts and People Using the IPsec Tunnel

Because the hosts and people using the IPsec tunnel are assumed to be using the organization's equipment and networks, existing policies regarding acceptable use of the organization's systems should already address most policy needs regarding IPsec tunnel use. Examples include host access requirements (e.g., authentication) and vulnerability mitigation requirements (e.g., patching OS and application vulnerabilities). Existing policy also typically specifies technical controls that must be used on each host, such as antivirus and antispyware software and a personal firewall, as well as the minimum acceptable configuration for the technical controls.

A.2 Communications with a Business Partner Network

In this scenario, an organization wants to establish an IPsec VPN to protect certain communications between a system on its network and a system on a business partner's network. This VPN would be created by having each organization deploy and manage an IPsec gateway on its own network, and configuring the gateways so that they protect communications between the organizations through an IPsec tunnel. This section focuses on the formal agreements made between the two organizations, and also summarizes policy considerations related to the organization's IPsec gateway and management server, and the people and hosts within the organization using the IPsec tunnel.

A.2.1 Interconnection Agreement

Federal policy requires Federal agencies to establish interconnection agreements for connections with business partners.[154] Specifically, OMB Circular A-130, Appendix III, requires agencies to obtain written management authorization before connecting their IT systems to other systems, based on an acceptable level of risk. The written authorization should define the rules of behavior and controls that must be maintained for the system interconnection, and it should be included in the organization's system security plan. It is critical that the organization and the business partner establish an agreement between themselves regarding the management, operation, and use of the interconnection, and that they formally

[154] NIST SP 800-47, *Security Guide for Interconnecting Information Technology Systems*, contains information on interconnection agreements, as well as extensive guidance on planning, establishing, maintaining, and disconnecting system interconnections, developing an interconnection agreement. It is available for download from http://csrc.nist.gov/publications/nistpubs/.

document this agreement. The agreement should be reviewed and approved by appropriate senior staff from each organization.

An interconnection agreement is typically composed of two documents: an Interconnection Security Agreement (ISA) and a Memorandum of Understanding or Agreement (MOU/A).[155] The ISA is a security document that specifies the technical and security requirements for establishing, operating, and maintaining the interconnection. It also supports the MOU/A between the organizations. Specifically, the ISA documents the requirements for connecting the systems, describes the security controls that will be used to protect the systems and data, contains a topological drawing of the interconnection, and provides a signature line. The MOU/A documents the terms and conditions for sharing data and information resources in a secure manner. Specifically, the MOU/A defines the purpose of the interconnection; identifies relevant authorities; specifies the responsibilities of both organizations; and defines the terms of agreement, including apportionment of costs and the timeline for terminating or reauthorizing the interconnection. The MOU/A should not include technical details on how the interconnection is established or maintained; that is the function of the ISA.

Items that are typically part of the ISA include the following:

- The information and data that will be made available, exchanged, or passed one-way only between the systems through the IPsec gateways, and the sensitivity of the information
- The services offered over the VPN by each organization, if any
- The user community that will be served by the VPN
- Description of all system security technical services pertinent to the secure exchange of data between the systems; examples include the use of FIPS 140-2 approved encryption mechanisms to protect communications, and the use of physical security controls to restrict access to the IPsec gateway devices and the systems
- Summary of the behavior expected from users who will have access to the interconnection; for example, each system is expected to protect information belonging to the other through the implementation of security controls that protect against intrusion, tampering, and viruses, among others
- Titles of formal security policies that govern each system
- Description of the agreements made regarding the reporting of and response to information security incidents for both organizations
- Explanation of how the audit trail responsibility will be shared by the organizations and what events each organization will log; should include the length of time that audit logs will be retained.

Items that are typically part of the MOU/A include the following:

- Description of the systems communicating through the VPN

[155] Appendices A and B of NIST SP 800-47 contain detailed guidance on developing an ISA and an MOU/A, as well as a sample of each. Rather than develop an ISA and MOU/A, organizations may choose to incorporate this information into a formal contract, especially if the interconnection is to be established between a Federal agency and a commercial organization. Also, in some cases, organizations may decide to use established organizational procedures for documenting the agreement, in lieu of an ISA and MOU/A.

- Discussion of the types of formal communications that should occur among the owners and the technical leads for the systems
- A statement regarding the security of the systems, including an assertion that each system is designed, managed, and operated in compliance with all relevant federal laws, regulations, and policies.

As a foundation for the interconnection agreement, the organization should have general policy statements regarding the appropriate and necessary use of IPsec, so that it is clear when and how IPsec should be used to protect an interconnection.

A.2.2 IPsec Gateway Devices and Management Servers

The organization should have policy statements that apply to the security and acceptable use of its IPsec gateway devices and management servers, as described in Section A.1.1.

A.2.3 Hosts and People Using the IPsec Tunnel

As described in Section A.1.2, existing policies regarding acceptable use and security of the organization's systems should already address most or all policy needs regarding IPsec tunnel use by hosts and people within the organization.

A.3 Communications for Individual Remote Hosts

In this scenario, an organization wants to establish an IPsec VPN to protect communications between individual remote hosts used by telecommuting employees and its main network. This VPN would be created by having the organization deploy and manage an IPsec gateway on its main network. Employees' computers would be configured with IPsec clients that would establish tunnels with the IPsec gateway as needed to protect communications between the laptops and the organization's main network. This section presents policy consideration examples for remote hosts and the organization's IPsec gateway and management server.[156]

A.3.1 Remote Access Policy

The organization should have a remote access policy that includes IPsec usage by employees from both organization-controlled and other systems. The organization might also choose to have each employee that will use the IPsec implementation to sign a remote access agreement or a copy of the remote access policy before being permitted to do so.[157]

IPsec-related items that are typically in a remote access policy include the following:

- Description of appropriate and inappropriate usage of the IPsec connection (e.g., forbidding personal use, forbidding use by other individuals)
- Pointers to other organization policies that apply to remote access, such as an acceptable use policy or a VPN policy

---

[156] Additional guidance on policy and security considerations for remote access users is available from NIST SP 800-46, *Security for Telecommuting and Broadband Connections*, available at http://csrc.nist.gov/publications/nistpubs/.

[157] The policy and agreement could also be used for non-employee use of the IPsec implementation. Depending on the details of the policy and agreement, some changes might be needed to make them suitable for addressing non-employee use.

- Remote access authentication requirements, such as two-factor authentication or strong passwords
- Requirements for the networking profile of remote hosts; for example, the policy might forbid a host from being connected to the organization's network and another network at the same time, as well as forbidding split tunneling
- Minimum hardware and software requirements for remote hosts, including acceptable operating systems and patch levels
- Required security controls for remote hosts, such as up-to-date antivirus and antispyware software and personal firewalls; could also include required configuration settings for the controls, such as scanning all files before placing them onto the host

Organizations might also wish to require remote hosts to be checked automatically for vulnerabilities, malware, or other security problems immediately after establishing an IPsec connection. This should be stated in the remote access policy.

A.3.2 IPsec Gateway Devices and Management Servers

The organization should have policy statements that apply to the security and acceptable use of its IPsec gateway devices and management servers, as described in Section A.1.1. In addition, the organization might add policy statements specific to IPsec usage by remote hosts, such as the following:

- Automatic termination and disconnection of idle connections after X minutes
- Requirement for creating and maintaining of a list of authorized users, disabling access for individual users as soon as it is no longer needed, and auditing the list of authorized users periodically.

Appendix B—Case Study Configuration Files

This section contains configuration files that are referenced in the Section 6 case studies.

B.1 Section 6.1 Case Study

The following lists the contents of one of the Cisco router configuration files used in the Section 6.1 gateway-to-gateway case study.

```
!
version 12.0
service timestamps debug uptime
service timestamps log uptime
no service password-encryption
!
hostname 2621
!
enable secret 5 $1$rMk2$5fPj5s3CvYE35OSW0qkLD.
!
ip subnet-zero
no ip finger
!
!
crypto isakmp policy 1
 authentication pre-share
 group 2
crypto isakmp key sharedkey address xx.xx.xx.xx
!
crypto ipsec transform-set auth2 esp-3des esp-sha-hmac
!
!
 crypto map test 10 ipsec-isakmp
 set peer xx.xx.xx.xx
 set transform-set auth2
 match address 133
!
interface FastEthernet0/0
 ip address xx.xx.xx.xx 255.255.255.0
 no ip directed-broadcast
 crypto map test
!
interface FastEthernet0/1
 ip address 192.168.1.1 255.255.255.0
 no ip directed-broadcast
!
ip classless
ip route 0.0.0.0 0.0.0.0 20.20.20.20
no ip http server
!
access-list 133 permit ip 192.168.1.0 0.0.0.255 10.30.50.0 0.0.0.255
!
line con 0
login
 transport input none
line aux 0
line vty 0 4
login
!
end
```

B.2 Section 6.2 Case Study

The following lists the contents of the OpenBSD server's configuration files, as described in the Section 6.2 host-to-gateway wireless network protection case study.

B.2.1 isakmpd.conf

```
[General]
Policy-file=            /etc/isakmpd/isakmpd.policy
Retransmits=            4
Listen-On=              192.168.0.100

[Phase 1]
192.168.0.27=           ISAKMP-peer-laptop1

[Phase 2]
Passive-connections=    IPsec-laptop1-server

[ISAKMP-peer-laptop1]
Phase=                  1
Transport=              udp
Local-address=          192.168.0.100
Address=                192.168.0.27
Configuration=          Default-main-mode
Authentication=         +dEwaCIO+LiEkPELIbSiH24U8719mtDy0KG86NrtCkQ=

[IPsec-laptop1-server]
Phase=                  2
ISAKMP-peer=            ISAKMP-peer-laptop1
Configuration=          Default-quick-mode
Local-ID=               server
Remote-ID=              laptop1

[Host-server]
ID-type=                IPV4_ADDR
Address=                192.168.0.100

[Host-laptop1]
ID-type=                IPV4_ADDR
Address=                192.168.0.27

[Default-main-mode]
DOI=                    IPSEC
EXCHANGE_TYPE=          ID_PROT
Transforms=             3DES-SHA

[Default-quick-mode]
DOI=                    IPSEC
EXCHANGE_TYPE=          QUICK_MODE
Suites=                 QM-ESP-3DES-SHA-SUITE
```

B.2.2 isakmpd.policy

```
KeyNote-Version: 2
Comment: This policy accepts ESP SAs from a remote that uses the right password
Authorizer: "POLICY"
Licensees: "passphrase: +dEwaCIO+LiEkPELIbSiH24U8719mtDy0KG86NrtCkQ="
Conditions: app_domain == "IPsec policy" &&
        esp_present == "yes" &&
        esp_enc_alg == "3des" &&
        esp_auth_alg == "hmac-sha" -> "true";
```

Appendix C—Glossary

Selected terms used in the guide are defined below.

Aggressive Mode: Mode used in IPsec phase 1 to negotiate the establishment of an IKE SA through three messages.

Asymmetric Cryptography: Cryptography that uses separate keys for encryption and decryption; also known as public key cryptography.

Authentication Header Protocol: IPsec security protocol that can provide integrity protection for packet headers and data through authentication.

Diffie-Hellman Group: Value that specifies the encryption generator type and key length to be used for generating shared secrets.

Encapsulating Security Payload Protocol: IPsec security protocol that can provide encryption and/or integrity protection for packet headers and data.

Hash Algorithm: Algorithm that creates a hash based on a message.

Internet Key Exchange Protocol: Protocol used to negotiate, create, and manage security associations.

IP Payload Compression Protocol: Protocol used to perform lossless compression for packet payloads.

Keyed Hash Algorithm: Algorithm that creates a hash based on both a message and a secret key; also known as a hash message authentication code algorithm.

Main Mode: Mode used in IPsec phase 1 to negotiate the establishment of an IKE SA through three pairs of messages.

Network Address Translation: A mechanism for mapping addresses on one network to addresses on another network, typically private addresses to public addresses.

Network Layer Security: Protecting network communications at the layer of the TCP/IP model that is responsible for routing packets across networks.

Packet Filter: Specifies which types of traffic should be permitted or denied and how permitted traffic should be protected, if at all.

Perfect Forward Secrecy: An option available during quick mode that causes a new shared secret to be created through a Diffie-Hellman exchange for each IPsec SA.

Pre-Shared Key: Single key used by IPsec endpoints to authenticate endpoints to each other.

Protection Suite: Set of parameters that are mandatory for IPsec phase 1 negotiations (encryption algorithm, integrity protection algorithm, authentication method, and Diffie-Hellman group).

Public Key Cryptography: Cryptography that uses separate keys for encryption and decryption; also known as asymmetric cryptography.

Quick Mode: Mode used in IPsec phase 2 to negotiate the establishment of an IPsec SA.

Security Association: Set of values that define the features and protections applied to a connection.

Security Association Lifetime: How often each SA should be recreated, based on elapsed time or the amount of network traffic.

Security Parameters Index: Arbitrarily chosen value that acts as a unique identifier for an IPsec connection.

Symmetric Cryptography: Cryptography that uses the same key for both encryption and decryption.

Transport Mode: IPsec mode that does not create a new IP header for each protected packet.

Tunnel Mode: IPsec mode that creates a new IP header for each protected packet.

Virtual Private Network: Virtual network built on top of existing networks that can provide a secure communications mechanism for data and IP information transmitted between networks.

Appendix D—Acronyms

Selected acronyms used in the guide are defined below.

3DES	Triple DES
AES	Advanced Encryption Standard
AES-CBC	AES-Cipher Block Chaining
AES-CTR	AES-Counter Mode
AH	Authentication Header
ALG	Application Layer Gateway
ARP	Address Resolution Protocol
BITS	Bump in the Stack
CA	Certification Authority
CBC	Cipher Block Chaining
CCMP	Counter-Mode/CBC-MAC Protocol
CHAP	Challenge Handshake Authentication Protocol
CMVP	Cryptographic Module Validation Program
CPI	Compression Parameter Index
CRL	Certificate Revocation List
DES	Digital Encryption Standard
DH	Diffie-Hellman
DHCP	Dynamic Host Configuration Protocol
DMZ	Demilitarized Zone
DNS	Domain Name System
DSA	Digital Signature Algorithm
DSL	Digital Subscriber Line
DSS	Digital Signature Standard
EAP	Extensible Authentication Protocol
EC2N	Elliptic Curve over $G[2^N]$
ECDSA	Elliptic Curve DSA
ECP	Encryption Control Protocol
ESP	Encapsulating Security Payload
FIPS	Federal Information Processing Standards
FISMA	Federal Information Security Management Act
FTP	File Transfer Protocol
GPG	GnuPG
GRE	Generic Routing Encapsulation
GSEC	Group Security
HMAC	Hash Message Authentication Code
HTTP	HyperText Transfer Protocol
HTTPS	HyperText Transfer Protocol Secure
ICMP	Internet Control Message Protocol
IDEA	International Data Encryption Algorithm

IDS	Intrusion Detection System
IGMP	Internet Group Management Protocol
IETF	Internet Engineering Task Force
IKE	Internet Key Exchange
IP	Internet Protocol
IPComp	IP Payload Compression Protocol
IPS	Intrusion Prevention System
IPsec	Internet Protocol Security
IPsec-WIT	IPsec Web Based Interoperability Tester
IRTF	Internet Research Task Force
IRC	Internet Relay Chat
ISA	Interconnection Security Agreement
ISAKMP	Internet Security Association and Key Management Protocol
ISP	Internet Service Provider
IT	Information Technology
IV	Initialization Vector
L2F	Layer 2 Forwarding
L2TP	Layer 2 Tunneling Protocol
L2VPN	Layer 2 VPN
L3VPN	Layer 3 VPN
LDAP	Lightweight Directory Access Protocol
MAC	Message Authentication Code
MD	Message Digest
MODP	Modular Exponential
MOU/A	Memorandum of Understanding or Agreement
MPPE	Microsoft Point-to-Point Encryption
MSEC	Multicast Security
MTU	Maximum Transmission Unit
NAT	Network Address Translation
NAT-T	Network Address Translation Traversal
NIC	Network Interface Card
NIST	National Institute of Standards and Technology
NVD	National Vulnerability Database
OCSP	Online Certificate Status Protocol
OMB	Office of Management and Budget
PAD	Peer Authorization Database
PAP	Password Authentication Protocol
PCP	IP Payload Compression Protocol
PFS	Perfect Forward Secrecy
PKI	Public Key Infrastructure
PPP	Point-to-Point Protocol
PPVPN	Provisioner-Provided VPN
PPTP	Point-to-Point Tunneling Protocol
QoS	Quality of Service

RADIUS	Remote Authentication Dial In User Service
RFC	Request for Comment
RMON	Remote Monitoring
SA	Security Association
SAD	Security Association Database
SCTP	Stream Control Transmission Protocol
SHA	Secure Hash Algorithm
SIP	Session Initiation Protocol
SMTP	Simple Mail Transfer Protocol
SP	Special Publication
SPD	Security Policy Database
SPI	Security Parameters Index
SSH	Secure Shell
SSL	Secure Sockets Layer
TACACS	Terminal Access Controller Access Control System
TCP	Transmission Control Protocol
TCP/IP	Transmission Control Protocol/Internet Protocol
TDEA	Triple Data Encryption Algorithm
TKIP	Temporal Key Integrity Protocol
TLS	Transport Layer Security
TTL	Time to Live
UDP	User Datagram Protocol
URL	Uniform Resource Locator
VoIP	Voice over IP
VPN	Virtual Private Network
VPNC	Virtual Private Network Consortium
WAN	Wide Area Network
WEP	Wired Equivalent Privacy
WPA	Wi-Fi Protected Access
XCBC	XOR Cipher Block Chaining
XOR	Exclusive OR

Appendix E—Resources

The lists below provide examples of resources that may be helpful in planning and implementing IPsec solutions.

Print Resources

Bollapragada, Vijay, et al., *IPSec VPN Design*, Cisco Press, 2005.

Doraswamy, Naganand and Harkins, Dan, *IPSec: The New Security Standard for the Internet, Intranets, and Virtual Private Networks (Second Edition),* Prentice Hall PTR, 2003.

Frankel, Sheila, *Demystifying the IPsec Puzzle,* Artech House, 2001.

Northcutt, Stephen, et al., *Inside Network Perimeter Security (Second Edition)*, Sams, 2005.

Shea, Richard, *L2TP: Implementation and Operation,* Addison-Wesley, 1999.

Tan, Nam-Kee, *Building VPNs with IPSec and MPLS*, McGraw-Hill, 2003.

Documents

Name	URL
FIPS 140-2, Security Requirements for Cryptographic Modules	http://csrc.nist.gov/publications/fips/fips140-2/fips1402.pdf
FIPS 197, Advanced Encryption Standard (AES)	http://csrc.nist.gov/publications/fips/fips197/fips-197.pdf
How to Use Internet Protocol Security to Secure Network Traffic Between Two Hosts in Windows 2000	http://support.microsoft.com/?kbid=301284
IPsec Product Technical Configuration Guidelines	http://www.icsalabs.com/icsa/docs/html/communities/ipsec/IPsec_Technical_Config_Guidelines.pdf
IPsec VPN Advanced Troubleshooting Guide	http://www.icsalabs.com/icsa/docs/html/communities/ipsec/IPsec_Advanced_Toubleshooting_GuideFinal.pdf
NIST SP 800-32, Introduction to Public Key Technology and the Federal PKI Infrastructure	http://csrc.nist.gov/publications/nistpubs/800-32/sp800-32.pdf
NIST SP 800-41, Guidelines on Firewalls and Firewall Policy	http://csrc.nist.gov/publications/nistpubs/800-41/sp800-41.pdf
NIST SP 800-46, Security for Telecommuting and Broadband Communications	http://csrc.nist.gov/publications/nistpubs/800-46/sp800-46.pdf
NIST SP 800-47, Security Guide for Interconnecting Information Technology Systems	http://csrc.nist.gov/publications/nistpubs/800-47/sp800-47.pdf
NIST SP 800-48, Wireless Network Security: 802.11, Bluetooth, and Handheld Devices	http://csrc.nist.gov/publications/nistpubs/800-48/NIST_SP_800-48.pdf
NIST SP 800-52, Guidelines for the Selection and Use of Transport Layer Security	http://csrc.nist.gov/publications/nistpubs/800-52/SP800-52.pdf
NIST SP 800-58, Security Considerations for Voice Over IP Systems	http://csrc.nist.gov/publications/nistpubs/800-58/SP800-58-final.pdf
NIST SP 800-67, Recommendation for the Triple Data Encryption Algorithm (TDEA) Block Cipher	http://csrc.nist.gov/publications/nistpubs/800-67/SP800-67.pdf

Name	URL
Problem Areas for the IP Security Protocols	http://www.research.att.com/~smb/papers/badesp.pdf
PSK Cracking Using IKE Aggressive Mode	http://www.ernw.de/download/pskattack.pdf
Step-by-Step Guide to Internet Protocol Security (IPSec)	http://www.microsoft.com/windows2000/techinfo/planning/security/ipsecsteps.asp

Resource Sites

Name	URL
Cryptographic Module Validation Program (CMVP)	http://csrc.nist.gov/cryptval/
FIPS-Approved Digital Signature Algorithms	http://csrc.nist.gov/cryptval/dss.htm
FIPS-Approved Symmetric Key Algorithms	http://csrc.nist.gov/cryptval/des.htm
GSEC Research Group	http://www.securemulticast.org/gsec-index.htm
ICSA Labs IPsec Community	https://www.icsalabs.com/ipsec
IETF IP Security Protocol (ipsec) Working Group	http://www.ietf.org/html.charters/OLD/ipsec-charter.html
IETF IP Version 6 Working Group	http://www.ietf.org/html.charters/ipv6-charter.html
IETF Transport Layer Security (tls) Working Group	http://www.ietf.org/html.charters/tls-charter.html
IPsec mailing list archive	http://www.vpnc.org/ietf-ipsec/
MSEC Working Group	http://www.securemulticast.org/msec-index.htm
NIST IP Security Web Based Interoperability Tester (IPsec-WIT)	http://ipsec-wit.antd.nist.gov/
NIST IPsec Project	http://csrc.nist.gov/ipsec/
NIST: Sample Practices, Policies, Checklists and Implementation Guides	http://csrc.nist.gov/pcig/
Virtual Private Network Consortium (VPNC)	http://www.vpnc.org/
VPN Protocols	http://www.vpnc.org/vpn-standards.html
VPNC Testing for Interoperability	http://www.vpnc.org/testing.html
Windows 2000 IPSec	http://www.microsoft.com/windows2000/technologies/communications/ipsec/default.asp

IPsec-Related Request for Comment (RFC) Documents

Name	URL
RFC 1828: IP Authentication Using Keyed MD5	http://www.ietf.org/rfc/rfc1828.txt
RFC 1829: The ESP DES-CBC Transform	http://www.ietf.org/rfc/rfc1829.txt
RFC 2085: HMAC-MD5 IP Authentication with Replay Prevention	http://www.ietf.org/rfc/rfc2085.txt
RFC 2104: HMAC: Keyed-Hashing for Message Authentication	http://www.ietf.org/rfc/rfc2104.txt
RFC 2401: Security Architecture for the Internet Protocol	http://www.ietf.org/rfc/rfc2401.txt
RFC 2402: IP Authentication Header	http://www.ietf.org/rfc/rfc2402.txt
RFC 2403: The Use of HMAC-MD5-96 within ESP and AH	http://www.ietf.org/rfc/rfc2403.txt
RFC 2404: The Use of HMAC-SHA-1-96 within ESP and AH	http://www.ietf.org/rfc/rfc2404.txt
RFC 2405: The ESP DES-CBC Cipher Algorithm With Explicit IV	http://www.ietf.org/rfc/rfc2405.txt
RFC 2406: IP Encapsulating Security Payload (ESP)	http://www.ietf.org/rfc/rfc2406.txt

Name	URL
RFC 2407: The Internet IP Security Domain of Interpretation for ISAKMP	http://www.ietf.org/rfc/rfc2407.txt
RFC 2408: Internet Security Association and Key Management Protocol (ISAKMP)	http://www.ietf.org/rfc/rfc2408.txt
RFC 2409: The Internet Key Exchange (IKE)	http://www.ietf.org/rfc/rfc2409.txt
RFC 2410: The NULL Encryption Algorithm and Its Use With IPsec	http://www.ietf.org/rfc/rfc2410.txt
RFC 2411: IP Security Document Roadmap	http://www.ietf.org/rfc/rfc2411.txt
RFC 2412: The OAKLEY Key Determination Protocol	http://www.ietf.org/rfc/rfc2412.txt
RFC 2451: The ESP CBC-Mode Cipher Algorithms	http://www.ietf.org/rfc/rfc2451.txt
RFC 2857: The Use of HMAC-RIPEMD-160-96 within ESP and AH	http://www.ietf.org/rfc/rfc2857.txt
RFC 3173: IP Payload Compression Protocol (IPComp)	http://www.ietf.org/rfc/rfc3173.txt
RFC 3526: More Modular Exponential (MODP) Diffie-Hellman Groups for Internet Key Exchange (IKE)	http://www.ietf.org/rfc/rfc3526.txt
RFC 3554: On the Use of Stream Control Transmission Protocol (SCTP) with IPsec	http://www.ietf.org/rfc/rfc3554.txt
RFC 3566: The AES-XCBC-MAC-96 Algorithm and Its Use With IPsec	http://www.ietf.org/rfc/rfc3566.txt
RFC 3602: The AES-CBC Cipher Algorithm and Its Use With IPsec	http://www.ietf.org/rfc/rfc3602.txt
RFC 3664: The AES-XCBC-PRF-128 Algorithm for IKE	http://www.ietf.org/rfc/rfc3664.txt
RFC 3686: Using AES Counter Mode with IPsec ESP	http://www.ietf.org/rfc/rfc3686.txt
RFC 3706: A Traffic-Based Method of Detecting Dead IKE Peers	http://www.ietf.org/rfc/rfc3706.txt
RFC 3715: IPsec-NAT Compatibility Requirements	http://www.ietf.org/rfc/rfc3715.txt
RFC 3884: Use of IPsec Transport Mode for Dynamic Routing	http://www.ietf.org/rfc/rfc3884.txt
RFC 3947: Negotiation of NAT-Traversal in the IKE	http://www.ietf.org/rfc/rfc3947.txt
RFC 3948: UDP Encapsulation of IPsec ESP Packets	http://www.ietf.org/rfc/rfc3948.txt

Other Request for Comment (RFC) Documents

Name	URL
RFC 1334: PPP Authentication Protocols	http://www.ietf.org/rfc/rfc1334.txt
RFC 1661: The Point-to-Point Protocol (PPP)	http://www.ietf.org/rfc/rfc1661.txt
RFC 1968: The PPP Encryption Control Protocol (ECP)	http://www.ietf.org/rfc/rfc1968.txt
RFC 2003: IP Encapsulation within IP	http://www.ietf.org/rfc/rfc2003.txt
RFC 2246: The TLS Protocol Version 1.0	http://www.ietf.org/rfc/rfc2246.txt
RFC 2341: Cisco Layer Two Forwarding	http://www.ietf.org/rfc/rfc2341.txt
RFC 2637: Point-to-Point Tunneling Protocol	http://www.ietf.org/rfc/rfc2637.txt
RFC 2661: Layer Two Tunneling Protocol	http://www.ietf.org/rfc/rfc2661.txt
RFC 2784: Generic Routing Encapsulation	http://www.ietf.org/rfc/rfc2784.txt
RFC 2818: HTTP Over TLS	http://www.ietf.org/rfc/rfc2818.txt
RFC 2888: Secure Remote Access With L2TP	http://www.ietf.org/rfc/rfc2888.txt
RFC 3078: Microsoft Point-to-Point Encryption (MPPE) Protocol	http://www.ietf.org/rfc/rfc3078.txt
RFC 3193: Securing L2TP Using IPsec	http://www.ietf.org/rfc/rfc3193.txt
RFC 3316: Internet Protocol Version 6 (IPv6) for Some Second and Third Generation Cellular Hosts	http://www.ietf.org/rfc/rfc3316.txt

Name	URL
RFC 3546: Transport Layer Security (TLS) Extensions	http://www.ietf.org/rfc/rfc3546.txt
RFC 3748: Extensible Authentication Protocol (EAP)	http://www.ietf.org/rfc/rfc3748.txt

Appendix F—Index

A

Access control, 2-4, 3-1
Advanced Encryption Standard (AES), ES-2, 2-4, 4-10
  AES-XCBC-MAC-96, 3-2
Aggressive mode, 3-15, C-1
Authentication, 2-3, 3-1, 3-11, 4-2, 4-8, 4-20
Authentication Header (AH), ES-1, 3-1, 3-23, C-1
  Packet header, 3-2
  Transport mode, 3-1, C-2
  Tunnel mode, 3-1, C-2
  Version 3, 3-4
Availability, 2-5

B

Broadcast traffic, 7-1

C

Compression Parameter Index (CPI), 3-19
Confidentiality, 2-3, 2-5
Cryptographic accelerator, 4-10
Cryptographic algorithm, 4-2, 4-10
  Asymmetric, 2-4, 2-9, C-1
  Encryption, 3-10
  Integrity protection, 3-11
  Symmetric, 2-4, 2-9, 3-6, C-2
Cryptographic Module Validation Program (CMVP), ES-2, 2-4
Cryptography
  Public key, 2-4, C-1

D

Diffie-Hellman (DH) group, 3-11, 3-17, 4-12, C-1
Digital Encryption Standard (DES), 2-4
Digital signatures, 3-11, 4-8

E

Encapsulating Security Payload (ESP), ES-1, 3-5, 3-23, C-1
  Transport mode, 3-6, C-2
  Tunnel mode, 3-5, C-2
  Version 3, 3-9
Encryption, ES-1, 3-1
Extensible Authentication Protocol (EAP), 3-18

F

Federal Information Processing Standards (FIPS), ES-2, 2-4
Federal Information Security Management Act (FISMA), 1-1

H

Hash algorithm, C-1
Hash message authentication code (HMAC), 2-4, 3-2
  HMAC-MD5, 3-2, 4-10
  HMAC-SHA-1, 3-2, 4-10
Header, 2-1

I

Initialization vector (IV), 3-7
Integrity, 2-3, 2-5, 3-1, 3-2
Integrity protection, ES-1
Interconnection Security Agreement (ISA), A-3
Internet Key Exchange (IKE), ES-1, 3-10, 3-23, C-1
  Aggressive mode, 4-12
  Group exchange, 3-17
  Informational exchange, 3-17
  Main mode, 4-12
  Phase one exchange, 3-10, 4-12
  Phase two exchange, 3-15
  Security Association (SA), 3-10
  Version 2, 3-18
Internet Protocol (IP)
  Version 6 (IPv6), 7-2
IP address, virtual, 4-7
IP header, 3-2
IP Payload Compression Protocol (IPComp), ES-2, 3-19, 3-23, C-1
IPsec, 2-3, 2-9, 3-1
  Alternatives, 4-2, 5-1
  Cryptographic algorithm, 4-20
  Deployment, ES-2, 4-1, 4-20
  Design, ES-2, 4-1, 4-2, 4-18, 4-19
  Implementation security, 4-18
  Interoperability, 4-16
  Management, ES-2, 4-1, 4-19, 4-20
  Needs, ES-2, 4-1, 4-19
  Packet filter, 4-2, 4-10, 4-20, C-1
  Planning, ES-2, 4-1, 4-19
  Policy, 4-3
  Protection suite, C-1
  Security Association (SA), 3-15
  Testing, ES-2, 4-1, 4-14, 4-20
IPsec architecture, 4-2, 4-3
  Gateway placement, 4-3
  Gateway-to-gateway, ES-1, 2-5, 2-8, 2-9, 3-20, A-1, A-2
  Host address space management, 4-6
  Host-to-gateway, ES-1, 2-6, 2-8, 2-9, 3-21, A-4
  Host-to-host, ES-1, 2-7, 2-8, 2-9, 3-1, 3-22
IPsec client software, 4-5

K

Key, 2-3
Keyed hash algorithm, 3-2, C-1

L

Layer 2 Forwarding (L2F), 5-2, 5-6, 5-7
Layer 2 Tunneling Protocol (L2TP), 4-4, 4-7, 5-2, 5-6, 5-7

M

Main mode, 3-10, C-1
MD5, 2-4
Memorandum of Understanding or Agreement (MOU/A), A-3
Message authentication code (MAC), 2-3, 3-2
Multicast traffic, 7-1

N

Network address translation (NAT), 3-2, 3-6, 4-4, C-1
  Discovery, 4-4
  Traversal (NAT-T), 4-4
Network layer security, 2-1

O

Office of Management and Budget (OMB) Circular A-130, 1-1

P

Padding, 3-7, 4-12
Payload, 2-1
Peer Authorization Database (PAD), 3-18
Perfect Forward Secrecy (PFS), 3-16, 4-12, C-1
Point-to-Point Protocol (PPP), 5-1
Point-to-Point Tunneling Protocol (PPTP), 5-2, 5-6, 5-7
Policy, A-1
Pre-shared keys, 3-11, 4-8, 4-18, C-1
Pretty Good Privacy (PGP), 2-2, 5-5
Protection suite, 3-10
Public key encryption, 3-11
Public key infrastructure (PKI), 7-2

Q

Quick mode, 3-15, C-2

R

Rekeying, 3-17
Replay, 2-3, 3-1
Replay protection, 3-3

S

Secure Hash Algorithm (SHA-1), 2-4
Secure Shell (SSH), 5-5
Security Association (SA), 3-2, 3-10, C-2
  Lifetime, 3-17, 4-12, C-2
Security Association Database (SAD), 3-16
Security Parameters Index (SPI), 3-2, 3-7, C-2
Security Policy Database (SPD), 3-17
Split tunneling, 4-5

T

Traffic analysis, 2-3
Transmission Control Protocol/Internet Protocol (TCP/IP), ES-1, 2-1, 2-8
  Application layer, ES-1, 2-1, 2-8
  Data link layer, ES-1, 2-1, 2-2, 2-9
  Network layer, ES-1, 2-1, 2-2, 2-8, C-1
  Transport layer, ES-1, 2-1, 2-2, 2-8
Transport Layer Security (TLS), 2-2, 5-3, 5-7
  Reverse proxy server, 5-3, 5-6, 5-8
Triple Data Encryption Algorithm (TDEA), ES-2
Triple Digital Encryption Standard (3DES), 2-4

U

UDP encapsulation, 4-4

V

Vendor ID, 3-14
Virtual private network (VPN), ES-1, 2-4, 2-9, C-2
  Application layer protocols, 5-5, 5-6, 5-8
  Architecture, ES-1
  Data link layer protocols, 5-1, 5-6
  Provisioner-provided, 5-3
  Transport layer protocols, 5-3, 5-6

www.ingramcontent.com/pod-product-compliance
Lightning Source LLC
Chambersburg PA
CBHW080300180526
45167CB00006B/2609